PAPIER MACHE

Miranda Innes

PAPIER MACHE

Photography by Clive Streeter

DK

DORLING KINDERSLEY
LONDON · NEW YORK · STUTTGART · MOSCOW

A DORLING KINDERSLEY BOOK

Created and produced by
COLLINS & BROWN LIMITED
London House
Great Eastern Wharf
Parkgate Road
London SW11 4NQ

Project Editor	Heather Dewhurst
Managing Editor	Sarah Hoggett
Senior Editor	Colin Ziegler
Art Director	Roger Bristow
Designers	Patrick Knowles
	Marnie Searchwell
	Steven Wooster
DTP Designer	Claire Graham
Photography	Clive Streeter

First published in Great Britain in 1995
by Dorling Kindersley Limited
9 Henrietta Street, London WC2E 8PS

A CIP catalogue record for this book is available
from the British Library.

ISBN 0 7513 0247 3 ✓

Reproduced by Daylight, Singapore
Printed and bound in France by Pollina – n° 67893 - A

Contents

Getting Started

Shaping, Moulding and Frameworks

Decorative Ideas and Finishes

Introduction

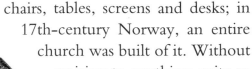

IF MESSING ABOUT in boats is the quintessence of pleasure for articulate water rats, squelching about with paper pulp is heaven for anyone whose childhood was too short, who never had long enough in the sandpit, or who is simply halfway dextrous and has a mind to make beautiful, quirky and amusing objects for the price of a daily paper.

Papier mâché is great for all sorts of reasons. To begin with, there is absolutely nothing so conducive of a pleasing sense of smugness as recycling rubbish; who knows, you may even get to read the newspapers that are forming your work of art. As a pastime, it is impeccably green, miraculously cheap and, if you make a disastrous bodge or your creation collapses, you can either use it as a firelighter or mulch your roses with it, launching yourself with a clear conscience into a new project using tomorrow's papers.

No material is so amenable or adaptable as papier mâché. In the 19th century, it was used to make

Fish Box
This colourful papier mâché container is enhanced by three-dimensional moulded fish motifs.

chairs, tables, screens and desks; in 17th-century Norway, an entire church was built of it. Without aspiring to anything quite so ambitious, you can easily make delicious frivolities like bangles, beads and brooches; or you can turn your hand to more serious and practical items, such as trays, bowls and clocks.

As a beginner in a hurry to become acquainted with the stuff, you can enjoy the textured rough and ready surface that comes naturally. Cast your mind back to the tactile pleasures and uncritical enthusiasm of nursery school pursuits: small children lose themselves in the task at hand, whether it be modelling clay men or making palaces of sand – the activity is more absorbing than the finished object – and this is a wonderfully liberating attitude. As you gain experience and can envisage the

Handmade Paper
A rainbow range of coloured, speckled paper.

creative possibilities of papier mâché, you can apply an alchemist's repertoire of cunning finishes to emulate the feel and look of lacquer, porcelain or even marble. You can

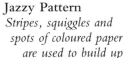

Jazzy Pattern
Stripes, squiggles and spots of coloured paper are used to build up a pattern.

use papier mâché to explore your long untapped creativity and make a few discoveries about yourself, or you can use it to keep a kitchen full of hyperactive children innocently occupied for a whole rainy weekend.

Papier mâché can be frisky and naive, or the same humble raw materials can undergo a miraculous transformation and make the smoothest, most subtle and sophisticated things you have ever seen. Using just a clay base, wire netting, wooden underpinning or simply a cardboard frame, you can make some huge and peculiar shapes – such as a pantomime horse, a witch's hat for hallowe'en night, angels' wings and haloes for the annual Christmas nativity play, masks for *mardi gras*. Alternatively, you can make tiny pieces of jewellery literally in a matter of minutes at the kitchen table, using nothing more arcane than cardboard, paper, paint and glue. You can attack your creation with an electric sander to flatten its bumps, emboss it with string or stitching, distress it and generally work out your aggression on it. The more refined can dye it, gild it, cover it with brilliants, or enchant and embarrass their friends with loving messages using their most calligraphic

Tissue Splendour
Tissue paper painted with metallic powders and oil paints make a decorative mille-feuille.

Conical Vase
A conical vase is decorated with copper Dutch metal leaf, laid onto gold size then rubbed in place.

flourishes. You can use tiny glass beads to create a twinkling rim, or big wooden ones attached with thongs of leather to make something that might have come out of Africa. Paper clips and sweet wrappers could be recycled to decorate your earrings, or you might develop a penchant for studs or eyelets.

Above all, papier mâché is good, clean, sticky, innocent fun. Cheap, disposable and easy to make, you can use it to make the most of high days and holidays, feast days and festivals. Celebrate Easter with painted chickens, Christmas with twinkling, gem-studded tree decorations, or a birthday with a brilliant monogrammed box. Papier mâché is whatever you want to make it – the only limits are those of your imagination. And it is a golden opportunity to regain your lost youth and those evanescent hours in the sandpit. Have fun!

Beautiful Baubles
Easy to make, these beads are a perfect introduction to papier mâché.

Basic Materials and Equipment

PAPIER MACHE is an extemely cheap pastime because its principal material is recycled newspaper. Many of the other basic materials and items of equipment you will need to get started – such as scissors, glue, cardboard, masking tape, pencils and crayons – can be found around the home. Other pieces of equipment you will find useful include a scalpel and cutting mat, chicken wire and modelling clay. Once you progress from the beginner stage and want to experiment with different finishes and decorations, there are a few things you will have to purchase, but these are not

Assorted paper

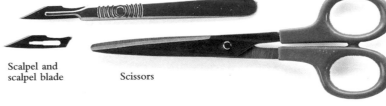

Scalpel and scalpel blade

Scissors

◀ Paper Selection
This is the essential ingredient for papier mâché; you can use newsprint, plain white cartridge paper or even brown paper for making pulp and layering, or coloured papers for a more decorative finish. You could also decorate your finished papier mâché with a selection of stylish patterned paper.

▲ Cutting Tools
A pair of sharp scissors and a lethally sharp scalpel are required for accurate cutting of cardboard to make cardboard frameworks. Take care when using a scalpel and always use a cutting mat.

Wallpaper paste

Rabbit skin glue granules

▶ Glues and Fixings
Use wallpaper paste or PVA glue for pasting on paper strips or for mixing with soaked paper to make paper pulp. Rabbit skin glue is an ingredient in gilding. Masking tape is used for reinforcing joins, and for attaching cardboard pieces together to make a framework.

PVA glue

Metal ruler

8

Masking tape

Soft cloth

Coloured crayons

prohibitively expensive. For example, you might need more unusual paper for decoration, a finer paintbrush for painting details, or a broader range of paints and metallic powders to give your papier mâché a special finish. All of these materials are readily available from most art shops.

▶ **Coloured Crayons**
Coloured crayons and pencils are a wonderful medium for decorating papier mâché. Easy to use and available in a wide range of colours, crayons also add a broken texture.

Pencils

Emulsion paint

▼ **Paints and Powders**
Most paints are suitable for decorating papier mâché, ranging from emulsion, acrylic, gouache and powder paint, to bole and metallic powder.

▶ **Pencils and Cloths**
Use pencils for drawing or tracing designs onto your papier mâché. Cloths are useful for absorbing water from wet pulp, and for polishing.

Absorbent cloth

Modelling clay

Corrugated cardboard

Powder paint

Bole

Metallic powder

Balloon

▼ **Paintbrushes**
Always choose the best brush you can afford. You will need a house-painter's brush, a varnishing brush and a few artist's brushes.

▶ **Bases and Frames**
You can use thick cardboard as a base for papier mâché, build frames from chicken wire and make moulds from modelling clay or balloons.

Thick cardboard

Assorted brushes

Chicken wire

Sandpaper

Getting Started

THE BEST THING about papier mâché is that you can start right now. You don't need complicated equipment, expensive materials or a degree in fine arts to begin. Mistakes don't matter a jot, and while perfection is a laudable ambition, it is by no means essential – you can turn out a very respectable and characterful bowl while you are getting the hang of the process. As your confidence grows, you can proceed to more demanding shapes and more exacting finishes.

To start with, nothing beats speed – kick off with something that you can finish today.

A tiny trinket bowl to learn about the different properties of layered paper and pulp, an angular vase that builds on a straightforward cardboard shape – these are the simple first principles from which all else follows. So put on your oldest shirt, forget the ironing and enjoy your paperwork.

Tissue Scraps

MATERIALS
2 pieces A1
cartridge paper
Water
PVA glue
Clingfilm

EQUIPMENT
Large bowl
Blender
Sieve
Cloth

See p.15 for materials
to decorate the bowl.

PAPIER MACHE is nothing if not adaptable – by using different techniques you can be bright and bold, or subtle and refined. This little bowl made of decorated pulp is at the more ethereal end of the spectrum, and exploits the delicate translucency of tissue paper with a confetti of tiny overlapping pieces speckled with gold, echoing the discreetly shimmering haze of gold, bronze and turquoise on the outside.

Once the potential of paper as a decorative material in its own right takes hold, you will see possibilities in the most unlikely places: different colours and qualities of tissue paper and fine handmade paper combine to give a different effect; natural wheat and straw colours mixed with gold and black speckles look very sophisticated, while more layers of toning blues and greens give depth and brilliance. Or you might use printed tissue as a collage, with decorative citrus fruit wrappers, the blue and white pictorial papers favoured by some French bakers to show off their baguettes, or bought tissue covered in extravagant blowsy roses – all torn into tiny pieces and attached to your bowl in an intricate jigsaw of abstract pattern.

Translucent Tissue
Tissue paper scraps layered in this bowl have the luminous translucency of a wash of watercolour paint. This is a fascinating way to exploit the huge range of newly available handmade dyed and textured papers. The interplay of technique and colour within and outside makes this bowl something of a subtle work of art.

Going for Gold
These two shimmering gold bowls achieve two different effects: for ultimate dazzle go for gold; to soften the effect decorate with tissue pieces for a bowl of beautiful scraps.

Making the Bowl

Paper pulp gives a very different texture from layering –
the even roughness has a tactile charm. A certain manpower
is necessary to give the pulp a regular thickness.

1 *Tear two pieces of A1 cartridge paper into small pieces about 2.5cm (1in) square and leave to soak overnight in a bowl of water. Taking a handful at a time and adding plenty of water, liquidize the soaked paper in a blender to make pulp. Strain the paper pulp over a bowl to remove excess water (see inset). The resulting pulp should be a spongy mass.*

2 *Add PVA glue to the sieved pulp in the proportion of approximately 30g (1oz) PVA glue to 500g (1lb) paper pulp. Mix the glue in with your hands until it is incorporated. The pulp mixture should now be spongy and silky to the touch.*

3 *Line your bowl with clingfilm and press a few handfuls of pulp into its base with the back of your fingers to compress the fibres and remove any air pockets. Build up the sides of the bowl, pressing with a dry cloth as you go (see inset) to remove excess water, until the pulp feels hard and damp to the touch. Make sure the thickness of the bowl is even all around.*

4 *After leaving it to dry in a warm place for a few hours, gently ease away the clingfilm from the edges of the mould. Carefully lift out the damp paper bowl and peel away the clingfilm. If any cracks or holes appear in the paper bowl, fill them in with damp pulp and smooth this over with your fingers. Leave the bowl to dry completely for a few days.*

Decorating the Bowl

Tiny, overlapping postage stamps of subtly coloured tissue decorate the inside of this gilded bowl, a translucent finish which is just right for such a delicate and fragile creation.

Decorated tissue paper

MATERIALS
Iridescent acrylic
paints
Non-tarnishing
wax gilt
Tissue paper
Gold ink
PVA glue
Metallic powder
Water

EQUIPMENT
Artist's brush
Cloth
Protective mask

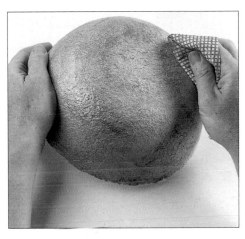

1 *Coat the inside of the bowl with a thin layer of iridescent white acrylic paint, and the outside with a thin layer of bronze. The paints will soak in and seal all the surfaces. Allow the paints to dry. Then, using a combination of pale gold, bronze and turquoise, paint the outside in a random manner and leave to dry for an hour.*

2 *Dip a soft dry cloth into non-tarnishing wax gilt, then rub it gently over the outside of the bowl. This will give the bowl a soft sheen.*

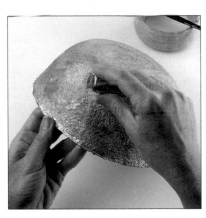

3 *Decorate pieces of tissue paper with dye or paint and leave to dry. Then spatter the paper with gold ink. First dip a brush in gold ink then, holding the brush over the paper, tap it against your hand to produce fine spatters, or flick the brush over the paper to produce larger spots. Finally, dab the brush randomly over the paper to produce large blobs. Leave to dry.*

4 *Tear the tissue paper into small pieces, approximately 2.5cm (1in) square. Using a dilute mixture of 1 part PVA glue to 1 part water, coat the inside of the bowl, then stick down overlapping pieces of tissue. Paste more dilute PVA on top of the tissue to seal. Then paste tissue pieces randomly in the same manner on the outside of the bowl, just beneath the rim. Allow the bowl to dry.*

5 *Paint PVA glue around the rim of the bowl and in the centre of the tissue paper squares on the outside of the bowl. Dust lightly with metallic powder. It is advisable to wear a mask to reduce the risk of inhaling the fine metallic powder.*

Tiny Starburst Bowl

MATERIALS

Cartridge paper
Water
Cold water fibre-
reactive dyes
Clingfilm
Paper varnish
(optional)

EQUIPMENT

Bowl
Blender
Sieve
3 small dishes
Spoon
Cloth
Varnish brush

THIS LITTLE JEWEL-LIKE BOWL is unusual in that the bold colours on the inside and outside of the bowl correspond with each other exactly. In terms of papier mâché, you cannot get much simpler than this formula, and the pulp technique is not difficult to master. The result has great charm, with its intense depth of colour and blurred bands of pattern.

Working with pulp gives an opportunity to experiment with different dyes, both subtle and bright, or the pastel shades which result from using ready-coloured papers. Small pieces of gold foil or thread can be incorporated in the process to give a finish of glittering richness, while a final coat of varnish will seal and protect the finished bowl and intensify the colour.

Little bowls like this look very pretty in groups – each one slightly different in colour, pattern and size from its neighbour. They make the perfect containers to cheer up and organize desk or dressing table paraphernalia. Like all papier mâché, they do not appreciate being wet – they would look very pretty in a fresh modern bathroom, but need several coats of varnish first to ensure they do not disintegrate.

Stars and Flowers
This pretty, featherweight bowl is built up from cartridge paper pulped in a blender and richly coloured with cold water fabric dye. This technique is unique because the pattern and colour are integral to the bowl and identical inside and out. The finished result has a lighthearted delicacy that could not be achieved by any other method.

Speckles, Stars and Spirals
Professional dyes produce the most intense colour, while commercial fabric dyes give a softer effect. You could omit the dyeing stage and use ready-coloured paper, which results in muted pastel colours.

Making the Bowl

Construction and decoration are part of the same process in this tiny, vibrant bowl. Nimble fingers and patience are necessary to keep colours separate and the pattern distinct.

1 *Tear a piece of A1 cartridge paper first into narrow strips and then into small pieces about 2.5cm (1in) square and leave to soak overnight in a bowl of water. This amount of paper will produce enough pulp to make three small bowls.*

2 *Add a handful of soaked paper to a blender and, adding plenty of water, liquidize the paper to make pulp. It may take a little while to liquidize all the paper as it is best to add only one handful of paper at a time, so as not to overload the blender. Strain the paper pulp over a bowl to remove excess water. The resulting pulp should resemble a spongy mass.*

3 *Divide the pulp into three containers. Make up cold water fibre-reactive dyes in yellow, pink and blue, following the manufacturer's instructions. Add drops of dye to each portion of pulp, mixing in well with a spoon. Leave to soak for several hours then rinse the pulp well. (If you prefer, you could use coloured papers to make the pulp and omit the dyeing stage. However, the colours will be less intense.)*

4 *Line a bowl with clingfilm. This will serve as the mould. Using a teaspoon, carefully arrange spoonfuls of yellow and pink pulp in the base of the mould to create a flower design. Then press the pulp gently with your fingertips to compress it and remove any air pockets.*

5 *Add spoonfuls of blue pulp to the mould to extend the design up the sides of the mould. As the pulp is quite sticky, it will cling to the sides of the mould and keep its shape. Keep turning the mould around as you add the pulp so that you can see the design from all sides. Continue to press the pulp gently with your fingertips or a teaspoon as you work.*

6 *Add further layers of pink and yellow pulp. Then, using a clean dry cloth, press the pulp carefully to compact the fibres and soak up the excess water collecting in the bottom of the bowl. Do not press too hard in case the pulp comes away from the sides of the mould. Repair any small gaps that may appear with pieces of pulp. Similarly, if a blob of pulp falls onto pulp of a different colour, simply remove it and patch up the design with the matching colour.*

7 *Continue adding pulp to build up the design until you reach the rim of the bowl. Then, using another dry cloth, press the pulp as hard as you can, working your way around the bowl, until the pulp feels hard and no longer wet.*

8 *Leave the bowl in a warm place, such as a sunny windowsill, to dry for a few hours. Then carefully ease away the clingfilm from the sides of the mould and lift out the paper bowl.*

9 *Peel away the clingfilm from the outside of the bowl and leave the bowl to dry out completely for a few days. Then, if you like, you can varnish it with paper varnish to deepen the colours.*

Brilliant Fishes

MATERIALS

Newsprint
Petroleum jelly
PVA glue
Water
Washing-up liquid
Modelling clay
Tissue paper
White emulsion
paint

EQUIPMENT

Dish to act as
mould
Cloth
Scissors
Cake rack
Scalpel
Small knife
Paintbrush

See p.23 for materials
to decorate the dish.

THE SIZZLING, high–intensity colour of this dish is a result of using opaque gouache paints. Gouache is an amiable medium, and lends itself to crisp detail and sharply defined decoration. Easily built up in the classic fashion from many layers of paper, the doughty solidity of this dish is enlivened by a three-dimensional sprinkling of shells. The more astrologically inclined might undertake a firmament of stars and moons, but there are many other simple and fashionable decorative motifs that can be adapted to add interest to an otherwise plain shape.

Layered papier mâché is justly renowned for its lightness and strength. Once you have achieved large oval and circular dishes, you might try turning your hand to a tray taken from an existing plastic version. Our Victorian forbears excelled in the fine art of papier mâché, and produced ornately shaped 'parlour-maid' trays to which they applied finely painted or découpaged flowers, layers of lacquer or lustrous pieces of abalone shell. Experiment and be inventive with your decoration.

Fin Extraordinaire
Wild subaqueous psychedelia with strange rainbow fishes and speckled shells on a purple and burgundy background freckled with gold. Opaque gouache paint allows the finest detail of fin and gill to be perfectly delineated.

Bowled Over
Anyone can manage quiet good taste – but accomplished kitsch is a much more exacting art. This bold and brilliant bowl is an exercise in unabashed extroversion, its entire surface richly decorated with skill and finesse.

Making the Dish

A simple shape brought to life with three-dimensional decorations moulded with modelling clay. It would be possible to use real shells if sculpting is beyond you.

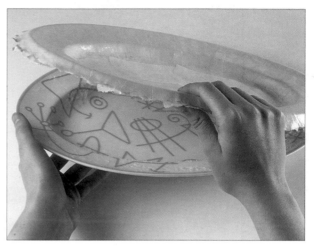

1 *Tear strips of newsprint about 5cm (2in) long. Rub a generous layer of petroleum jelly over the surface of the dish. Then, using dilute PVA glue (3 parts PVA to 1 part water), paste on strips of paper, overlapping as you go. Repeat the process, applying about 15 layers in all. Leave to dry for 48 hours.*

2 *Carefully ease back the rim of the paper dish, working your way around the edge, and peel it away from the mould. Clean the underside with a soft cloth and washing-up liquid to remove all traces of petroleum jelly. Trim the edges of the dish with scissors, following the line of the rim on the underside.*

3 *Make three shells out of modelling clay, each approximately 5cm (2in) long and 2.5cm (1in) wide, or to fit the rim. On each shell, rub petroleum jelly over one side at a time and, using dilute PVA glue, paste several layers of tissue paper over the surface. Leave to dry and repeat the process until you have built up about 30 layers.*

4 *After leaving the shells to dry on a cake rack for 48 hours, cut each shell in half with a scalpel. Scoop out the modelling clay with a small knife – it should come out easily if plenty of petroleum jelly was used earlier. Scrape out any remaining modelling clay to leave the paper shell halves clean.*

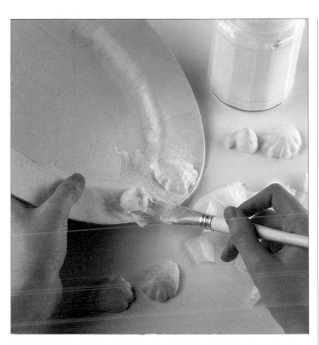

5 Using dilute PVA glue, stick the paper shell halves onto the rim of the paper dish. Hold the shells in position for a few minutes until they are secure. Then paste three layers of tissue paper over the shell shapes and leave to dry overnight.

6 Apply a coat of white emulsion paint over the entire dish and leave to dry. This will provide a smooth surface for decorating.

Decorating the Dish

A thick coat of emulsion – the poor man's gesso – smooths out the paper edges and makes a grateful surface for precise gouache fish of unknown species. Crib designs for fish, birds or butterflies from library nature books.

MATERIALS	EQUIPMENT
Gouache paints	Artist's brush
Spray varnish	Pencil
Gloss interior wood varnish	Tracing paper

Using gouache paints, paint a fish design onto the dish. If you do not feel confident enough in your freehand skills, find suitable images in a book and, having photocopied them to the desired size, transfer them onto the dish with tracing or carbon paper. Paint the background in blue gouache to represent the sea, then paint each fish in a variety of bright colours. Paint the rim in a contrasting colour and finally paint the shells. Leave to dry, then apply one coat of spray varnish to fix the gouache. Finally, paint on two thin coats of gloss interior wood varnish for a tough shiny surface, allowing the varnish to dry between coats.

Tricorn Vase

MATERIALS
Thin cardboard
Mountboard
Masking tape
Wallpaper paste
Newsprint
Ready-mixed filler

EQUIPMENT
Pencil
Tracing paper
Cutting mat
Metal ruler
Scalpel or craft knife
Teaspoon

See p.27 for materials
to decorate the vase.

C RISP, ELEGANT ANGULAR LINES give this vase a sculptural quality. It has no affinity with fluffy flowers: if its contents have to be floral, spiky dried eryngium heads would suit or, alternatively, skeletal twigs, festooned with a string of tiny white fairy lights for an unsentimental nod to Christmas.

One advantage of a surface of flat planes is that it is ideal for collage – photocopied musical scores, possibly dipped in tea for fake antiquity, have the right kind of graphic appeal.

The artist who designed this vase has used the appliance of science – or geometry at least – to achieve more ambitious projects, such as a handsome fire surround with mantelpiece, and a gilded three-legged table. Both have an air of theatrical panache, and, while the former might be a fire hazard and the latter might not be load-bearing, they dramatically expand the repertoire of paper and glue.

Verdigris Vase
Using a geometric cardboard base gives this vase a strong masculine look unusual with papier mâché. Its bronzy-verdigris finish would be perfectly at home with modern furniture in a cool, uncluttered interior.

Graphic Appeal
The flat planes of the basic shape make an ideal surface to show off photocopied images and text in a graphic black and white collage. Or black and silver can be paired for sophistication.

Making the Vase

*A geometric approach to the imprecise art of papier mâché,
carefully cut and scored mountboard gives an unusually
decisive shape, in contrast to the more usual irregularities.*

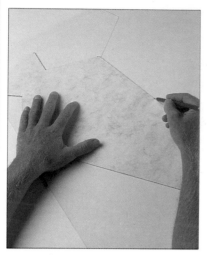

1 *Enlarge the template on p.92 to the required size, trace it onto thin cardboard, and cut it out. Draw around the template three times on mountboard, with the long sides of the template placed next to each other, so that you have one pencilled shape.*

2 *Place the mountboard on a cutting mat and, using a metal ruler and a scalpel or craft knife, carefully cut around the outline of the pencilled shape.*

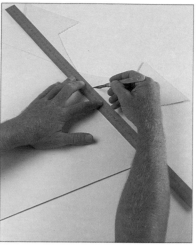

3 *Draw a pencil line along the base of the vase neck and, using a scalpel and metal ruler, score along these lines to make them easier to fold and give a sharper crease. Score along the side edges of the vase in the same way.*

4 *Turn the mountboard over and score along the narrow part of the vase neck in the same way as before. Mountboard with a black underside is recommended as a dark interior will give the vase a more finished look.*

5 *Fold the sides of the vase in to make a three-sided shape and tape together with masking tape. Bend in the folds of the neck and then tape these together. Aim for a close fit, but slight inaccuracies do not matter at this stage.*

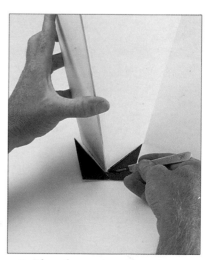

6 *Place the constructed vase on cardboard and cut around the edges to make a base. Tape the base to the bottom of the vase.*

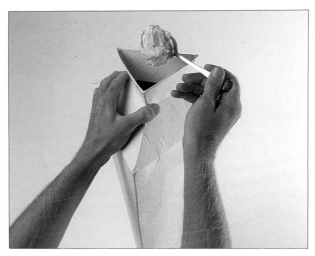

7 *Using wallpaper paste, stick 15 × 7.5cm (6 × 3in) strips of newsprint or brown paper over the vase to cover it entirely. Allow to dry then repeat with a further layer of paper strips. Leave to dry overnight. It is best not to use smaller strips of paper than these, as they will make the mountboard frame soggy and possibly misshapen, and create more lines on the finished vase.*

8 *Mix up a small amount of ready-mixed filler following the manufacturer's instructions, then insert two tablespoonfuls inside the vase to weight the base and help the vase stand upright. Check that the filler drops to the base and does not stick to the sides of the vase – if it does stick to the sides, simply shake the vase until the filler drops down to the base.*

Decorating the Vase

Tinting emulsion paint produces some extraordinary luminous colours. Here the gilding emphasizes the edges of the paper strips, and the coat of boot polish and bronze tones down the turquoise and gold.

Bronze powder

Boot polish

MATERIALS
White emulsion paint
Phthalo-green acrylic paint
Boot polish
Bronze powder
Hair spray

EQUIPMENT
Housepainter's brush
Cloth

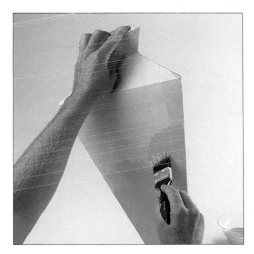

1 *Paint a coat of white emulsion over the papered vase. Leave to dry and then apply a coat of phthalo-green acrylic paint mixed with white emulsion. Here the colour was obtained by mixing 1 part acrylic paint with 2 parts emulsion paint. Leave the painted vase to dry thoroughly.*

2 *Dip a soft cloth first in boot polish and then in bronze powder. Then smear it quickly and lightly over the dry painted surface of the vase to leave random bronze patches over the vase, with the green colour still showing through. To fix the bronze powder, spray the vase with hair spray.*

Opalescent Bowl

MATERIALS

Cardboard
Balloon
String
Newsprint
PVA glue
Water
Sawdust
Whiting
Linseed oil
Wallpaper paste
White emulsion
paint, casein or gesso

EQUIPMENT

Plate, or pair of
compasses
Scissors
Craft knife
Flowerpot
Housepainter's
brush
Bowl

See p.31 for materials
to decorate the bowl.

EVERYONE LIKES BOWLS. There is something rotundly satisfying about the shape and they can be modelled upon existing bowls, balloons or even footballs. The basic shape can be played with in a variety of ways to make a rounded, egg-shaped or cylindrical body, with a ragged or smooth edge and a splayed or crimped lip. Decorate your bowl with string patterns, silver paper, silver studs, jewels or other *objets trouvés* and stand it on three globular feet or a solid base made from a collar of cardboard.

Having done all this, you can launch into the surface decoration of your bowl. Texture comes from glass-smooth gesso or the rustic rasp of sawdust. Colour can be solidly matt, or you can use layers of transparent inks or pearlized paint for a swirling, nacreous quality. You can add gold leaf, folksy potato prints or precise penlines, and give it an ancient air with antiquing or crackle varnish. In fact, life can be a bowl of just about anything you fancy.

Metallic Effect
Black ink makes its opalescent heart gleam darkly, almost like pewter; flakes and shreds of Dutch metal are scattered about its collar, and dark aquamarine matt paint is buffed to bring out its full intensity around the outside of this quirky and appealing bowl.

Bowl of Contrasts
As fragile as a peony and as tough as leather, the delicate gilded exterior of this bowl contrasts dramatically with the powerful orange-red colouring inside.

Making the Bowl

A quick and easy way to make a footed bowl. Use pulp thickened with sawdust for a deliberately irregular organic look, enhanced by the undulating rim.

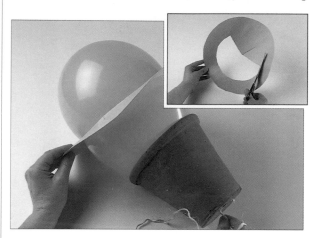

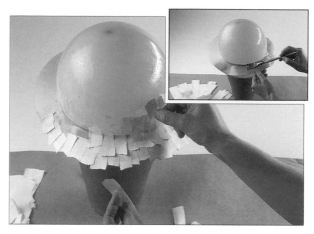

1 Using a plate or pair of compasses, cut a circle out of cardboard the required diameter of the outer rim. Cut a cross in the centre with a craft knife, then cut out the inner circle (see inset). Blow up a balloon inside the rim and tie a knot in the end. Secure with a length of string and thread it through the hole in the base of an earthenware flowerpot for support.

2 Having torn the newsprint into small pieces, cover the balloon and rim with PVA glue (see inset). Apply a line of pieces along one third of the outer edge of the rim. Then work up over the rim and to the top of the balloon in overlapping rows. Repeat this process until the surface of the balloon is completely covered.

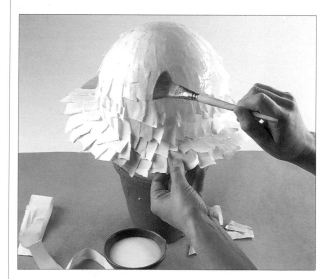

3 Paint glue generously over the balloon and rim, smoothing from top to bottom to expel air bubbles. Repeat the layering and gluing to build up three or four layers. Hang the bowl up by the string in a warm place – it will take about one hour to dry over a warm oven. As it dries, the rim will go wavy. Pop the balloon and remove it from the bowl.

4 To make paper pulp, tear up four double sheets of newsprint and make into pulp as in steps 1 and 2 on p.18. Add an equal part sawdust, ½ part whiting, 3 teacups PVA glue and 2 tablespoons linseed oil. Mix and sprinkle over wallpaper paste to absorb excess moisture. Apply the pulp evenly over the inside and rim of the bowl, smoothing it out well with wet fingers.

5 *Dry the bowl in a cool oven. Cut a narrow strip of cardboard and glue or tape the ends together to make a small circle. Place this on the bottom of the bowl and fill with pulp, pressing down evenly.*

6 *When dry, trim the excess paper from the rim with scissors and paint the bowl inside and out with white emulsion paint, casein paint or gesso.*

Decorating the Bowl

Pearlized acrylic ink is used here to give a glowing, translucent effect, heightened by gold Dutch metal leaf on the rim.

Gold Dutch metal leaf

MATERIALS
Pale turquoise pearlized acrylic ink
Darker turquoise transparent acrylic ink
Diluted black ink
Polyurethane varnish
Gold Dutch metal leaf
Beeswax

EQUIPMENT
Artist's brush
Paper towels
Cloth

1 *Cover the inside and rim of the bowl with pale turquoise pearlized ink. When dry, paint darker turquoise ink on the outside and streak it over the rim.*

2 *Rub diluted black ink on the inside of the bowl, then rub down the outside and inside with crumpled paper towels for a distressed effect.*

3 *Paint the rim with varnish and, when touch-dry, apply gold Dutch metal leaf torn into small pieces. Rub down with the ball of the thumb or a crumpled paper towel. Finally, polish the bowl with a cloth dipped in beeswax to build up a protective patina.*

Well Urned

MATERIALS

Newsprint
Water
PVA glue
Wallpaper paste
Linseed oil
Petroleum jelly
Masking tape
White emulsion paint
Acrylic and metallic paints
Coloured crayons
Fixative
Satin spray varnish

EQUIPMENT

Large bowl
Blender
Sieve
Garden urn for mould
Craft knife
Housepainter's brush
Artist's brush

PAPIER MACHE HAS MANY VIRTUES — it is lightweight, cheap, durable and adaptable. It can be used to make tiny beads and huge containers equally successfully — and even if you do have a complete disaster and your work of art collapses in a heap of pulp, you can chuck it away and start again with a clear conscience. So, do not be afraid to tackle sizeable objects, such as this beautiful urn. As long as you have something to act as a mould, there is nothing to stop you. Here the shape was taken from a garden urn; the layered paper and pulp were carefully cut away in two halves, and then stuck together again — a perfectly respectable method which allows you to make use of more complex shapes and to explore life beyond the bowl. Try using existing vases, bottles, lamp-bases and candlesticks as moulds — narrow necks are not a problem. If you are feeling particularly creative, you might experiment with a lamp-base (weighted with dried beans for stability) and give it a matching shade.

Colourful Trio
Handsome containers for walking sticks and umbrellas or the perfect receptacles for fake sunflowers, this trio of sunny-coloured urns look good together as variations on a theme. Make sure that the bases are weighted and very thoroughly sealed if they are likely to get damp.

1 *Make paper pulp (see p.13), using 12 sheets of newsprint, 8 tablespoons PVA glue, and 2 teaspoons each of wallpaper paste and linseed oil. Cover the sides of the mould with petroleum jelly, then with newsprint. When dry, smooth on pulp, 1cm (½in) thick. Dry for a week then repeat for the base.*

2 *Using a sharp craft knife, cut the moulded pulp in half down the length of the urn. Gently ease one pulp half away from the mould. You might find it helpful to use a spatula here. If any pieces of pulp break off, don't despair — simply stick them back in place with PVA glue.*

3 *Stick the pulp halves together using PVA glue. Wrap masking tape around the outside to secure. Paste two layers of newsprint dipped in dilute PVA glue over the urn. When dry, paint it with white emulsion, then decorate with paint and crayons (see p.51) and, when dry, spray with fixative and varnish.*

Ideas to Inspire

S hown on the following pages is a range of papier mâché bowls and plates – all different in style, shape, design and size – to inspire the budding artist. Now that you have learned the basics of making a bowl, experiment with some of the ideas suggested here; alternatively, take a moulding technique from one, add a clever use of beads from another and make something that is truly, inimitably, your own.

▶ **A Class Menagerie**
Made from paper pulp using a bowl as a mould, these bowls take the theme of animals and birds. Simple shapes are repeated around the inside, decorated with acrylics and crayon over an emulsion base, while the rims are highlighted in gold.

▼ **Jagged Edges**
Jagged cardboard rims were taped to the bowl edges and held in place with glued paper. The bowls were coated with a white emulsion/PVA mix, then painted in blue and orange acrylics and decorated with ripped paper.

▼ **Sunflower Bowl**
Made from layering paper over a mould and then taping on irregular cardboard shapes for the petals, this bowl was painted with acrylic paints and then decorated with torn circles of paper and ink to create the sunflower seeds.

▲ **Starfish Plate**
The starfish shapes were painted gold and the plate was decorated with torn paper, painted green then spattered with gold.

▶ **Patchwork Bowls**
Inspired by Aboriginal art, these bowls were made from pulp using a cardboard mould; the feet, consisting of a trio of marble-sized balls of pulp, were attached with glue. The bowls were decorated with gouache and watercolours with gold leaf around the rim, and the spiral was decorated with sweet papers.

◀ **Gilded Bowls**
The crusty edge to these bowls was formed by leaving the wet pulp ragged at the rim. The bowls were painted inside and out with iridescent acrylics, and the rims were decorated with gold leaf. Finally, parts of both the inside and outside of the bowls were also decorated with gold leaf.

36

▲ **African Inspiration**
*Made from pulp, coloured
only by the newsprint and sugar
paper used to make it, these bowls
were pressed into plaster moulds to create an
ethnic pattern. The addition of chunky, wooden
beads around the rim, attached with beading twine
through holes drilled in the papier mâché, completes
your own personal tribal artefact.*

Shaping, Moulding and Frameworks

···

HAVING MASTERED THE BASICS
and built up an impressive
collection of bowls, you may
want to make something
rather more grandiose and altogether more
challenging. Papier mâché is a miraculously
versatile medium. It can be built up over a
wire base to make three-dimensional
sculptures; it can be layered over a cardboard
shape for strength and texture; you can
shape it over metal, ceramic, plastic or
plaster; or you can shape it like clay to
make your own version of baroque mouldings.
Once you have explored its plastic possibilities,
nothing will be safe from a thorough papering.
With a bit of wire netting or a sheet
of cardboard, you can conquer
the third dimension.

Jazz-time Clock

MATERIALS
Double corrugated
cardboard
PVA glue
Wallpaper paste
Paper

EQUIPMENT
Pair of compasses
Pencil
Scissors
Craft knife
Cutting mat
Paintbrush

See p.43 for materials
to decorate the clock.

TIMES HAVE CHANGED since the family grandfather clock ruled the hours. Clock mechanisms are now easy to come by and ridiculously cheap, so that you can design a different clock for every room in the house, or make a special occasion clock to commemorate a golden wedding or a 21st birthday.

Your clock can be any shape you wish. You might want something grand to grace your sitting room mantelpiece – columns, perhaps, with a square marbled face and discreet gilding. For your bedroom, disporting cherubs, photocopied and découpaged, might help you to wake with a smile on your face.

Clock numerals do not need to be spelt out: you could time your soufflé by a clock whose hands are carrots and whose numerals are radishes, or your hours can be marked by shells or sequins, autumn leaves, or numbers photocopied from typeface books or torn from newspapers.

Rose Window Clock Face
Strong, glowing colours, as bright as a stained glass window, enliven a clock face that has brilliantly transcended its humble origins. Indigo, purple, magenta, cerulean blue and fir green are not chosen for discretion, but for fun. Zigzags, spots, stars: papier mâché is a blank canvas upon which to experiment, and an invitation to have a good time.

New Faces
Anything with a flat front can become a clock – a circle, triangle or square. You can stand it on little feet and use Victorian engravings or wrapping paper as decoration if your design skills fail you.

Making the Clock

A classy way to recycle old cardboard boxes, extravagantly layered in three chunky dimensions. Precision cutting is helpful, but not essential, and you can alter size and shape to suit your whim.

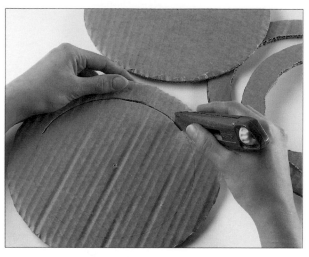

1 *Using a pair of compasses, draw four circles approximately 15cm (6in) in diameter on a piece of double corrugated cardboard. In the centre of three of these circles draw another circle, measuring approximately 10cm (4in) in diameter.*

2 *Cut out all four circles from the cardboard, then cut out the inner circles from three of these circles. It is easiest to use scissors to cut the outer circles, and a craft knife to cut the inner circles. When using a craft knife, protect your work surface with a cutting mat.*

3 *Pasting PVA glue between each layer, sandwich the four circles together in the following order: two cut-out circles, one solid circle, then one cut-out circle. Place a heavy weight on top of the glued circles, and leave to dry for about two hours.*

4 *Mix the wallpaper paste according to the manufacturer's instructions. Tear paper into strips approximately 5cm (2in) long and 2.5cm (1in) wide. Dip the strips one at a time into the wallpaper paste and stick the strips onto the "clock", smoothing them with your fingers. Overlap the layers as you go, and apply two layers on both sides of the clock before leaving it to dry.*

Decorating the Clock

Coloured paper comes in an irresistible rainbow range, and has a pleasant speckled texture – all of which you can exploit to the full, with lively additional spots and squiggles of your own.

Medium-weight paper in
assorted colours

MATERIALS
PVA glue
Medium-weight paper
in assorted colours
Water-based gloss
varnish
Clock movement and
hands
Rapid epoxy resin

EQUIPMENT
Cocktail stick
Drill

1 *Using dilute PVA glue (2 parts PVA glue to 1 part water), paste small overlapping strips of coloured paper onto the top and underside of the clock to cover the base completely.*

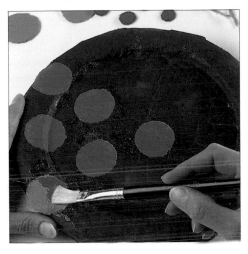

2 *Cut circles out of the coloured paper and paste these in a random pattern over the base on the front of the clock. There is no need to let the base dry first.*

3 *Paste on pieces of different coloured paper to build up the pattern. Use a cocktail stick to hold narrow strips of paper in place. Here triangles and small circles have been decorated with squiggles and dots. Leave the clock to dry overnight. Then apply a coat of water-based gloss varnish to protect the surface.*

4 *Turn the clock over so that the decorated side faces downwards and drill a hole in the centre of the clock back large enough to accommodate the shaft of the clock movement. Glue the clock movement in place with rapid epoxy resin applied both to the clock mechanism and to the back of the clock.*

5 *Cover the clock hands with coloured paper by pasting PVA onto the clock hands and placing them on a piece of coloured paper. Tear the paper around the hands, fold the torn paper edges over the back and glue them down to secure. Finally, fix the clock hands to the shaft of the clock movement and screw the centre piece over the hands to secure.*

Curtained Mirror

MATERIALS
Plastic sheet
Mirror
Chicken wire
Picture hanging wire
Newsprint
Wallpaper paste
White photocopy
paper

EQUIPMENT
Wire cutters
Ruler

See p.47 for materials
to decorate the
mirror frame.

A STUNNING EXAMPLE of the dramatic potential to be found in humble chicken wire and newsprint, this piece of *trompe-l'oeil* displays – aside from your face – a wonderful vigorous humour. Such a frame could cheer your outlook on the greyest Monday morning.

Building the design up with a photocopier gives you unlimited possibilities: you could use pages from Leonardo da Vinci's notebook, repeated images of fleurs-de-lis or botanical engravings culled from a graphic sourcebook. Enlarging and reducing, darkening and refining motifs gives them an interesting quality. If you have access to a colour photocopier, the visual world is yours to exploit. You could make a personal design from a collage of your past using wrapping paper, Valentines, postcards, ribbons, pressed flowers and skeleton leaves. Or you could base a freehand design on the elegant intricacies of Elizabethan embroidery. Once you start looking, you will see inspiration everywhere.

Tapestry Effect
A fabulous fake: newspaper and chicken wire drapery that falls in the extravagant folds of a piece of medieval tapestry – an effect that rich colours, bold patterns and matt varnish would emphasize.

Material Differences
Bronze, gold, mole brown and cinnabar – warm rich colours for a candle-lit mirror that exploits the sculptural possibilities of chicken wire.

Making the Mirror Frame

A wire armature enables you to create whatever sculptural shape takes your fancy – and because of the lightness and cheapness of the materials, size is no problem.

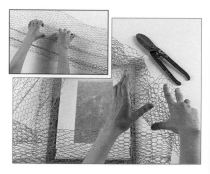

1 Tape a plastic sheet over the mirror to protect it. Cut a piece of chicken wire larger than the mirror. This mirror is 38 × 25cm (15 × 10in) and the wire 45 × 90cm (18 × 36in). Lay the mirror on top of the wire so that it is 33cm (14in) from the bottom. Fold up the lower edge of the wire over the mirror base by 1cm (½ in), then fold it back towards you to secure the mirror base. Fold the wire underneath itself to make a shelf at the base of the mirror.

2 Using wire cutters, make a cut into both sides of the chicken wire at the top and bottom edge of the mirror. Fold the wire in towards the mirror on each side, then fold it back out after securing the mirror by 1cm (½ in). Repeat with the top edge of the mirror and tuck under the wire ends to neaten.

3 Cut out another piece of chicken wire measuring 130 × 45cm (52 × 18in) for the drape, and bunch it into loose folds along its entire length (see inset). Arrange the wire drape around the mirror, pulling and manipulating it into shape. When you are satisfied with its appearance, secure it in position around the mirror by snipping individual wires along its length and folding them around the base wire.

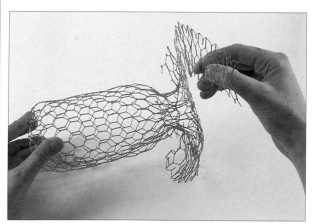

4 To make the vase, cut a piece of wire measuring 23 × 26cm (9¼ × 10½in) and roll it into a cylinder shape. Tuck the wire ends under at the base of the cylinder and fold the ends back slightly at the top to make the vase neck. Cut another piece of wire measuring 45 × 5cm (18 × 2in) for the rim and attach this to the neck of the cylinder shape. Secure it to the shelf of the mirror frame. Then attach a piece of picture hanging wire to the back of the mirror frame.

5 Using large squares of newsprint dipped in wallpaper paste, cover the front of the wire frame with a layer of newsprint, smoothing the paper down as you go. Repeat with a layer of white photocopy paper. When pasting paper strips next to the mirror, stick the paper to the mirror to secure it in place. Allow the front of the frame to dry, then repeat the process on the back.

Decorating the Mirror Frame

*One of the unsung stars of modern technology, the
photocopier is a powerful tool for designers. Here repeat
patterns are used to bold effect.*

Painted paper

MATERIALS
Paper to be patterned
and painted
Colour washes
Wallpaper paste
Gouache paint
(gold and copper)
Black wash
Satin polyurethane
varnish

EQUIPMENT
Artist's brush
Paper towel
or sponge
Varnish brush

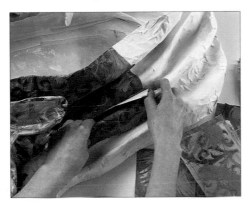

1 *Make sheets of patterned paper by
drawing a design in black and white.
Photocopy it enough times to cover the frame.
Apply different colour washes over the sheets
of paper and decorate with squiggles of gold
and daubs of colour. Tear the sheets into large
squares. Dip the patterned pieces of paper in
wallpaper paste, then paste onto the drape of
the mirror frame, keeping matching colours at
the same level on both sides of the drape to
give the effect of a real curtain. Then cover the
vase with a layer of patterned pieces of paper.*

2 *Paint the shelf of the mirror frame in
black paint and leave to dry. Then apply
a wash of gold paint over the top and allow to
dry again. Daub decorative gold dots onto
the vase.*

3 *Using copper gouache paint, paint
spots on the vase and add stripes
across the drapes and around the edges
for a stylish trim. Dip a scrunched-up
paper towel or a sponge in copper
gouache, dab it on paper to get rid of
the excess paint, then dab it all over
the shelf to create a textured pattern.*

4 *Using a very dilute black wash,
paint shadows in the folds of the
drapes and on the vase. The amount
you need to use will depend on the
brightness of the colours in your
decoration. If you have used bright
colours, you may need to add more
black shading than if you have used
pale colours. Leave the frame to dry.*

5 *Paint the back of the mirror frame
with black paint, shading in the
edges around the frame. Leave to dry.
Varnish the entire mirror frame for a
satin finish, then, when the frame is
dry, peel off the plastic sheet protecting
the mirror.*

Elephant Pot

MATERIALS
Thick cardboard
tube
Thick cardboard
Pencil
PVA glue
Newsprint
White emulsion paint

EQUIPMENT
Scissors
Ruler
Sandpaper
Paintbrush
Craft knife

See p.51 for materials
to decorate the pot.

A HINT OF THE EXOTIC and the warm colours of a Moorish market – yellow ochre, burnt cinnamon and rich turquoise blue – characterize this container. It possesses a high degree of finesse and uses sophisticated colouring, although the basic technique of building upon an existing cardboard shape simplifies matters. Its surface is evenly tactile, almost like ceramic or gesso, and there is not a bump or a wrinkle in sight – a refinement that requires patient smoothing when applying the paper. Containers using these more subtle colours look good massed together: a collection of harmonizing pots and jars of different sizes is very handsome.

The decorative motifs on the pot are simple blocked shapes whose outlines can easily be stencilled or traced from an image in a book. Elegant lettering and numerals also take to this finish very well. The technique of building on a cardboard foundation can be adapted to make wider or larger containers such as Shaker-style boxes or tall painted umbrella-stands, using cardboard cylinders of different sizes.

The Lid Fits
This little cylindrical container has the answer to wobbly or ill-fitting lids, with its snug liner that holds the top firmly in place. It is easily and quickly made, using existing cardboard tubing, covered with glass-smooth layers of newspaper. Its resulting quiet sophistication is unusual for papier mâché objects where theatrical exuberance is more the norm.

Pots of Colour
The liveliness of the colour comes from the brushed texture of the underlying emulsion, and the contrasts between crayon, acrylic paint and the opaque bands of gold.

Making the Pot

Sturdy little cylinders to hold kitchen tools, paintbrushes,
make-up tools and desk-top paraphernalia are utter simplicity
to make, using any size of cardboard tube as a foundation.

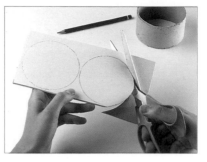

1 *Cut three sections from a cardboard tube measuring 7.5cm (3in), 6.5cm (2½ in) and 5cm (2in) respectively. The largest section will form the base of the pot and the other two pieces will make the lid. Rub the edges of each section with sandpaper to neaten.*

2 *Stand one of the tube sections on a piece of thick cardboard and draw around the base twice. Cut out the two circles. These will form the base and lid of the pot.*

3 *Taking the middle-sized tube section, cut down the length of the tube and trim off a strip approximately 6mm (¼ in) wide. Discard the strip and close the cut edges together to give the tube section a smaller circumference. Insert this section inside the smaller tube section, as shown, to make the pot lid.*

4 *Paste PVA glue around one rim of each tube section and glue the two cardboard circles onto these rims to create the base and lid of the pot.*

5 *Tear one large sheet of newsprint into strips approximately 12.5cm (5in) long and 2.5cm (1in) wide. Dip the strips one at a time into dilute PVA glue (3 parts PVA to 1 part water) and then paste the paper over the surface of the cardboard pot, smoothing it down with your fingers as you go. Cover the two halves of the pot inside and out, except for the lip of the lid, and leave to dry. Then paste on a second layer of newsprint strips and allow to dry again.*

Decorating the Pot

Use different kinds of paint and crayon together to give your pot a vivacious finish.

MATERIALS
Crayons
Acrylic paint
Silver metallic paint
Fixative
Household varnish

EQUIPMENT
Pencil
Paintbrush
Varnish brush

6 *Using a craft knife, score along the edge of the lip of the lid and peel off a thin layer of cardboard all around. The layer should be approximately half the thickness of the cardboard. Smooth down the lip with sandpaper to neaten. This will enable the lid to fit easily into the base of the pot.*

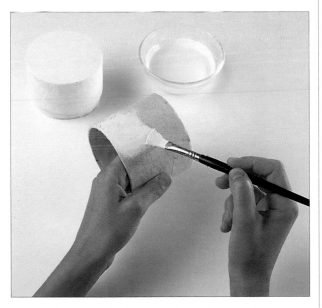

7 *Apply a coat of white emulsion paint over the two halves of the pot, both inside and out. Allow to dry and then paint on a second coat. The emulsion will provide a better surface than cardboard for decorating.*

Draw a design in pencil around the outside of the pot. Fill in the pencil outline with a combination of crayon and paint for subtle textural effects. Here the elephants and stars are crayoned while the background is painted in acrylic paint. Extra decoration is provided by narrow strips of silver metallic paint around the rim and base of the pot. Allow the paint to dry, then spray the pot with fixative, taking care not to inhale any. Apply a coat of varnish.

Kitsch Casket

MATERIALS

Thin cardboard
Corrugated cardboard
Masking tape
PVA glue
Water
Newsprint
Tissue paper
Modelling clay
Petroleum jelly
Rapid epoxy resin
White
emulsion paint

EQUIPMENT

Pencil
Scalpel
Metal ruler
Jam jar
Paintbrush
Cake rack
Spatula

See p.55 for materials
to decorate the casket.

T HIS CONTAINER is the perfect expression of the irreverent fun to be had with papier mâché in triumphant tribute to St Valentine's Day. Use the casket to hold wildly expensive chocolates, an amethyst engagement ring on a scarlet velvet cushion, or a collection of ribbon-bound love letters. For a more demure look, one could take seaside colours, and attach moulded starfish or real shells to the top and sides to make the perfect home for seaside souvenirs.

The box is too glorious to hold anything as banal as seed-packets or tax receipts, but a small collection of significant ephemera as an evolving diary to remind you of parties, proposals and passionate attachments is quite in order. If your courage fails you, it is perfectly permissible to simplify the design. Make your box without feet or double lid or even moulded hearts. You can then build cautiously from your successes, and, if a plain box turns out to be manageable, you might boldly proceed to tackle something rather more demanding.

A Labour of Love
Built up from a somewhat complex cardboard base, this box has been very carefully designed, despite its look of carefree insouciance. Three-dimensional moulded motifs and painstaking paintwork in exuberant colours combine in a container in which to keep your most precious possessions.

Inspired by Fish
The same shape and fishy inspiration with very different results: the black box sets off a kaleidoscope of vibrant clashing colour, beside which the shell-studded seaside casket looks almost quietly naturalistic.

Making the Box

Precise cutting and sticking are essential for the architectural finesse of this casket, and result in a stunning labour of love, the perfect home for billets-doux.

1 *Make six templates (see pp.92–3) from thin cardboard. Draw around the templates on corrugated cardboard and cut out the required number of pieces (you should have 16 in total). For neat edges, use a scalpel held against a metal ruler. Cut the corner edges of the box sides at 45°. This will help the pieces to fit together more easily when you assemble the box.*

2 *Assemble the box and lid following the diagram shown on p.93. Hold the pieces of cardboard in place with strips of masking tape.*

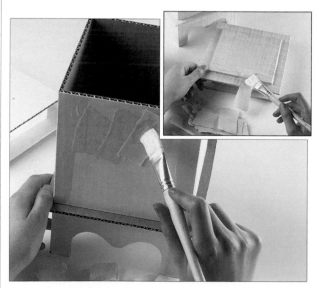

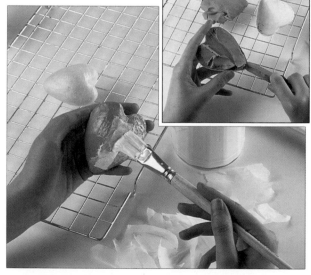

3 *Prepare the glue and paper. In a jam jar, mix 3 parts PVA glue with 1 part water. Tear strips of newsprint and tissue paper about 2.5 × 5cm (1 × 2in). Dipping a brush in the dilute PVA mixture, paste a layer of overlapping newsprint strips over all the edges and joins of the box and lid (see inset). Paste both the surface of the box and on top of the paper to ensure it lies flat. Continue until the box is covered, then leave to dry for 48 hours.*

4 *Make two hearts out of modelling clay approximately 5cm (2in) wide and 2.5cm (1in) thick, and a smaller heart approximately 4cm (1½ in) wide and 2cm (¾ in) thick. Cover with petroleum jelly then, using PVA glue, paste 30 layers of tissue paper over them in the same way as in step 3, p.22. Leave the hearts to dry on a cake rack for 48 hours, then remove the modelling clay in the same way as in step 4, p.22 (see inset).*

Decorating the Box

Leave your inhibitions behind and enjoy yourself – every millimetre of the surface should be alive with vibrant colour.

MATERIALS
Gouache paints
Spray varnish
Gloss interior wood
varnish

EQUIPMENT
Artist's brush
Varnish brush

5 *Cut out four cardboard heart shapes using the templates (see p.93). Glue one to each side of the box using dilute PVA. Glue a papier mâché heart half onto each cardboard heart; keep two of the larger heart halves for the lid. Then paste three layers of tissue paper over the heart shapes and leave them to dry for 24 hours.*

6 *To make a handle for the lid, cut out an arrow approximately 15cm (6in) long from cardboard (see template on p.93). Paste a layer of tissue paper over the arrow and sandwich it between the two remaining heart halves so that the arrow points downwards. Paste six layers of tissue paper over the heart and arrow to secure, and leave to dry for 24 hours.*

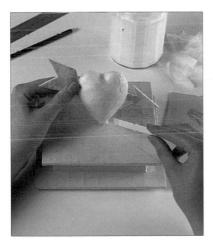

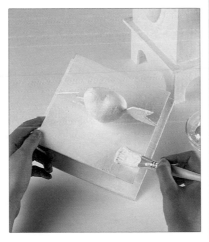

7 *Using a ruler and pencil, draw diagonal lines from corner to corner across the lid of the box to find the centre point. Using a spatula, apply rapid epoxy resin to the base of the heart handle and the centre point of the lid and glue the heart handle to the lid. Prop the heart in place for about ten minutes. Paper over the join with tissue paper when dry. Leave to dry for 24 hours.*

8 *Apply a coat of white emulsion paint over the box and lid, both inside and out, and leave to dry. This will provide a smooth surface for decorating.*

Decorate the box using gouache paints. First apply the base coats, varying them on each side of the box; here the colours used were ochre, red, purple and violet. Allow to dry, then paint red-brown and black squiggles over the top to create a leopard-skin pattern. Decorate the red and purple areas with gold spots and squiggles. When the paint is dry, apply one thin coat of spray varnish to fix the surface of the gouache and allow to dry. Finally paint on two thin coats of gloss interior wood varnish for a tough, shiny surface, allowing the varnish to dry between coats.

Carnival Mask

MATERIALS

Cardboard
Masking tape
Newsprint
PVA glue
Water
Modelling clay
Petroleum jelly
Gesso

EQUIPMENT

Pencil
Scissors
Scalpel
Paintbrush
Sandpaper

See p.59 for materials
to decorate the mask.

A MODEL MADE FROM cardboard shaped with modelling clay is used as the mould for this exuberant *mardi gras* mask. The clay face is smoothed over with many layers of newspaper strips to make the refined sculptural curves, and three coats of gesso are used to strengthen the papier mâché and give a sandable receptive surface for brilliant work with acrylic paint.

This method offers a wonderful opportunity for made-to-measure personalized masks for parties, Greek dramas, childrens' theatre or to hang on your walls as slightly sinister trophies of particularly memorable masked balls. This is your chance – exploit it with caution – to indulge in kindly caricature, and to give free rein to your decorative whims. Few people will object to being represented as a glorious bird of paradise complete with a tremulous tiara of feathers – but you may lose friends if you portray them in the guise of platypus or pig.

Decorative Disguise

A brilliant piece of bravura painting, this finely detailed, feathered mask is too good to waste on a single party, however magnificent, and would make a handsome, if startling, object to hang on your wall. Or it could be just the excuse you need to make a trip to Venice at carnival time.

Two Faces of Paper

Acrylic paint is perfect for fine brushwork. These two masks seem to come from an earlier age – the blue bird could grace a renaissance bal masqué, while the sun-bright lion has a strong heraldic flavour.

Making the Mask
Sculpted from modelling clay and cardboard, this fearsome mask could be adapted to make many different faces — beaks and snouts are just a matter of altering the cut and shape.

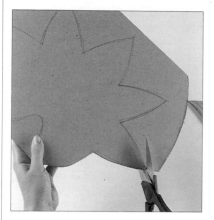

1 *Draw the shape of the mask on cardboard, and then draw the shape of a beak. Cut out both shapes with scissors.*

2 *Position the beak on the mask so that it juts out from the mask at an angle of 90°. Anchor it in place with two pieces of cardboard, taped first to each side of the beak and then to the mask.*

3 *Cover the taped cardboard where the beak joins the mask with torn strips of newsprint, pasted on with a dilute mix of 1 part PVA glue to 1 part water. This will strengthen the join and make it firm. Leave to dry for at least a day.*

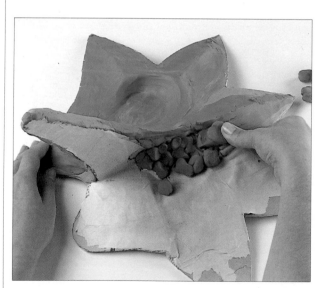

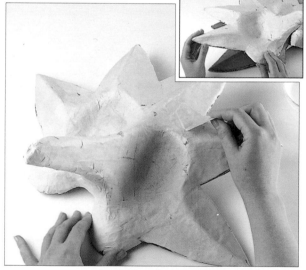

4 *Cover the surface of the mask with small lumps of modelling clay and smooth them down to define the shape of the mask. Build up the features such as the shape of the beak and hollows for the eyes. Be bold when modelling as fine details will be painted.*

5 *Cover the clay with petroleum jelly and paste 10 layers of newsprint on the front and back of the mask using dilute PVA glue as before. Leave to dry for approximately three days or until the mask is hard and dry. Using a scalpel, cut around the outer edges of the mask and along the length of the beak. Gently peel the mask away from the mould (see inset).*

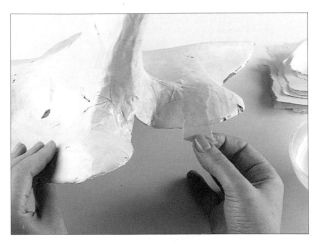

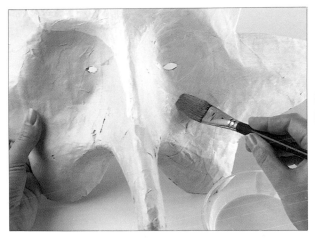

6 *Make eye holes and holes at the sides of the mask for threading ribbon through. Close the slit in the beak so that it fits snugly and tape the edges together with masking tape. Then paste strips of newsprint over the join and around the edges of the mask to smooth any rough areas.*

7 *Paint the mask with three coats of gesso, allowing each coat to dry before applying the next. The gesso will provide a good surface to paint on and it also strengthens the papier mâché. When dry, rub the gesso with sandpaper to give it a smooth finish.*

Decorating the Mask

Acrylic paint brings a carnival brightness and intensity of colour and allows the finer details of eye and brow to be sharply delineated.

Feathers

MATERIALS
Pale-coloured pencil
Acrylic paints
Feathers
Newsprint
PVA glue
Interior varnish
Ribbons

EQUIPMENT
Artist's brush
Varnish brush

1 *Using a pale-coloured pencil, draw the design onto the mask. Do not use an ordinary lead pencil because it might smear when you apply the paint. Apply the acrylic paints, using pale colours first and gradually building up layers of colour. Keep the paint fairly watery and, for greater texture, rub the paint into the gesso with your fingers.*

2 *Continue to paint the mask, progressing to darker, stronger colours, such as red and dark green. When you have finished painting the front of the mask, paint the reverse black. Allow the paint to dry, then attach the feathers to the back of the mask at the top with a few strips of pasted newsprint. Allow to dry, then varnish the mask with interior varnish for a glossy finish and protective coat. Finally, thread ribbons through the side holes and use these to tie the mask around your head.*

Ideas to Inspire

By using cardboard, wood, modelling clay, or chicken wire, you can create any shape you want. Included on the following pages are frames, bowls, clocks and dolls, and even a lifelike cockerel. Plunder the repertoire to make a Noah's ark or a lamp-base, and work your way up to carnival masks and side tables.

▶ **Nursery Dolls**
The heads of these dolls are scrunched-up balls of paper; the limbs and necks are plastic straws, covered with paper, which are joined to the stuffed cotton bodies with thread. Details were painted with acrylic, while the clothes were made from scraps of fabric.

◀ **Spherical Vases**
Moulded on a beach ball, these vases were painted with a mixture of emulsion and PVA glue, then painted with acrylics and scumbled with a cloth. Cut-out paper shapes were glued on for further decoration.

◄ Heraldic Frame
Built from a cardboard framework, this frame was painted with cream and blue acrylic, and rubbed back with sandpaper. The fleurs-de-lis and lettering were treated in the same way.

► Love Chest
A battered old chest was layered with coloured paper and torn strips of pages from romantic novels. When dry, it was painted with emulsion paint mixed with gouache in shades of pink, light blue, purple, silver and gold, then rubbed back with sandpaper and varnished.

▲ Shell Clock
Built from recycled cardboard, this clock was covered with mottled handmade paper, then decorated with stencilled shells.

◄ Wreath Frame
This frame was decorated with paper roses and polystyrene leaves, and given an oil-scumbled glaze.

▶ Toy Bug
This inventive toy bug was made by layering paper over a clay and plaster mould. A simple wind-up mechanism was attached to the underside. When pulled, the bug races across the floor.

▶ Starry Frame
Starry card shapes were glued onto this wooden frame and layered with paper. The frame was painted with white emulsion and PVA, then blue gouache, and rubbed with wet cotton buds. Gold paint was used for highlights.

▼ Fish Box
Made by layering paper over a clay and cardboard mould with paper pulp for detail, this container was decorated with gesso and acrylics then rubbed with wax.

▼ Rainbow Fish
This fish was constructed using a plaster mould. When dry, the fish was covered in gesso, sanded until smooth and then painted with acrylics, using first pale colours, then darker, stronger colours, and lastly gold acrylic. Finally, the fish was given a coat of floor varnish.

▲ Goldfish
This wire fish was decorated with cartridge paper, then coated with PVA and varnish.

◄ **Paper Poultry**
*A wire mesh structure
was used as a base for
this cockerel. The
shape was built up
with layers of paper
coated with wallpaper
paste. When dry, the
cockerel was painted
with acrylics and
finally varnished. The
effect is so lifelike that
some of the artist's real hens
have had to look twice!*

▼ **Giant Fish Plaque**
*Measuring 93cm (37in) long
and 50cm (20in) wide, this
plaque was constructed by
layering newsprint in a plaster
mould. When dry, the
mould was prised off and
the fish given four coats
of gesso, sanded until
smooth, and then
decorated with acrylics
and varnished.*

Decorative Ideas and Finishes

·······································

YOU'VE GOT TO GRIPS with the preliminaries, and can now indulge in the fine art of fancy decoration. This is where your imagination can run wild; you can cover your papier mâché with gesso for a porcelain-smooth finish; discover the splendour conferred by Dutch metal and gold leaf, or the satisfying antiquity that crackle glaze emulates; experiment with stitching and embossing, or decorate with glitter or glass jewels. Be bold and sassy with outrageous colour, or use more natural colours with shells and coloured glass as ornamentation.

Remember that no matter how many old newspapers you recycle this way, next Sunday will bring a fresh deluge to contend with.

Butterfly Tray

MATERIALS

Hardboard,
2mm (⅛ in) thick,
or mountboard
Cardboard
PVA glue
Masking tape
Cellulose paste
Newsprint

EQUIPMENT

Scissors
Matchstick
Paintbrush

See p.68 for materials
to decorate the tray.

THE JAPANESE do not have a monopoly on tea. With a bit of effort and a dash of style, you can create your own tea ceremony in recollection of better and more civilized times. Fine translucent china cups, a flowery teapot, buttered crumpets and a bouquet of butterflies on an artfully painted and aged tray will bring a touch of summer to fireside feasts.

This is your chance to exploit the pleasures of découpage, or the inspired use of the colour photocopier. A large flat surface is an invitation to have fun; with practice you will soon produce something pretty and personal. Try painting a freehand *trompe-l'oeil* of buns and biscuits, découpage a prim potted auricula from wrapping paper, try your hand at calligraphy to make an inscribed anniversary present, or stencil a chrysanthemum and splatter it in gold. You have the world on a tray.

Picnic Tea
Never mind the weather — a tray of butterflies will bring a scent of high summer, buddleias and blossom to the most wuthering winter. Découpage is fun and easy to do, and begs to be used as a lasting reminder of past pleasures: a wedding can be celebrated with valentine hearts and cherubs, while a sunny summer holiday can be remembered with shells and tropical fish.

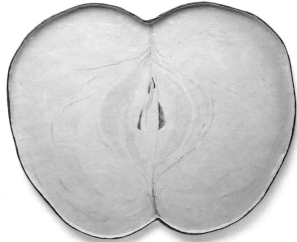

Autumn Harvest
Once smitten, you will find all sorts of unexpected things make terrific colour photocopies: fiery autumn leaves, with possibly a pheasant's feather and a fern frond will summon the season of mists and woodsmoke; or take your inspiration from autumn apples for a fruity looking tray.

Making the Tray

Papier mâché can be combined with anything. Here,
hardboard is given a thin veneer of paper for character.

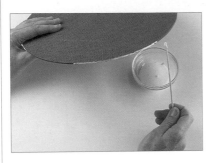 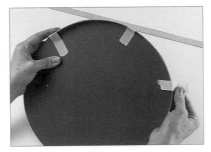 

1 *Cut a circle, about 30cm (12in) in diameter, from thick hardboard or mountboard. Cut a strip of cardboard, approximately 1.5cm (⅝in) wide and long enough to go around the edge of the circle. You may find it easier to cut two strips and then attach them separately. Using a matchstick or cocktail stick, apply PVA glue around the edge of the hardboard circle.*

2 *Attach the strip of cardboard to the edge of the hardboard circle to make the rim of the tray (the smooth side of the hardboard should be facing upwards). Hold the strips in place with masking tape as you go. Join the two edges of the cardboard neatly when you complete the circle. Paint the underside of the tray with a coat of PVA glue to seal and waterproof it. Leave the tray to dry thoroughly.*

3 *Using cellulose paste, paste thin strips of newsprint over the rim of the tray, wrapping them from the inside to the outside of the rim and pressing them down firmly into the joint. Paste larger strips of newsprint over the base of the tray until the whole tray is covered. Repeat to cover the tray with a second layer, and leave the tray to dry. Apply two more layers of paper and allow to dry.*

Decorating the Tray

All you need for découpage is a spirit of ruthless
plagiarism, a good pair of scissors and a pot of glue.

MATERIALS
Gesso tinted
with pigment
Acrylic paint
Paper motifs
cut from magazines
Paper glue
Acrylic high-build
découpage varnish
Dark-coloured
wax polish

EQUIPMENT
Medium-grade
sandpaper
Housepainter's brush
Medium- and coarse-
grade wire wool
Scissors
Paper towels
Artist's brush
Varnish brush
Cloth

1 *Lightly sand all surfaces of the tray to remove any uneven bumps. Then apply three layers of gesso tinted with pigment, allowing the tray to dry between coats. Lightly sand the tray before applying the last coat.*

2 *Paint random patches of three or four colours of acrylic paint over the surface of the tray – here white, yellow, green and burgundy. Mix and merge the colours together for a subtle summery effect and allow the tray to dry thoroughly.*

3 *Gently rub the tray with sandpaper to allow some of the gesso base to show through the paint. Then rub medium-grade wire wool over the surface.*

4 *Place the paper motifs upside-down on a paper towel, brush with paper glue (see inset), then place them glue-side down on the surface of the tray in a design of your choosing. Using a scrunched-up paper towel, blot the glued paper motifs thoroughly to absorb any excess glue and to remove any air bubbles. Any fine details can be painted onto the tray at this stage. Allow to dry.*

5 *Apply a minimum of six layers of varnish to the tray, allowing each layer to dry before applying the next. The rim and underside of the tray should have an extra three layers of varnish for protection. When the varnish is dry, rub coarse-grade wire wool over the surface of the tray in a circular motion. This will remove some of the shine and cover the surface with random scratches.*

6 *Using a soft cloth, rub dark-coloured fine wax polish into the scratch marks on the surface of the tray. Allow the polish to dry for approximately three-quarters of an hour, then rub off with a clean cloth. The dark-coloured polish will remain in the cracks to give the tray an aged and worn appearance*

Opulent Earrings

MATERIALS

Thick cardboard
Rapid epoxy resin
Earring findings
Newsprint
Wallpaper paste
White emulsion paint

EQUIPMENT

Pencil
Scissors
Matchstick
Bowl
Cake rack
Paintbrush
Pliers

See p.73 for materials
to decorate the
earrings.

THESE EARRINGS deliver a high dose of drama but, unlike the Koh-i-noor diamond, they need not hide in the safe when they are not adorning your ears. They are a glorious example of the wit and inventiveness that modern jewellery designers are bringing to their craft. They are also cheeringly simple to make, and invite experiment and variation.

The creator of these earrings also makes magnificent bangles and brooches, building on a basic shape of twisted paper for the former, and using a cardboard foundation for the latter. Having succeeded with the earrings, you could turn your hand to sets of co-ordinated theatrical jewellery to match particular outfits. Try personalizing a pair of earrings to make an unforgettable birthday present for a friend. Or celebrate special occasions with custom-made creations. Christmas, for example, might bring you out in the classic colour combinations of red, green and gold; scarlet and magenta hearts could be just the thing for Valentine's Day; or a favourite brocade jacket might suggest earrings and a brooch that pick up its colours and motifs. Above all, this kind of jewellery is great fun to make and should be worn in the same spirit.

Thrifty Glitter
Projecting a quite disproportionate degree of glamour, thanks to their witty, glittery finish, these earrings are easy to make. They do not pretend to be anything precious, just a bright kaleidoscope of gold paint, foil and gemstones.

Hearts and Stars
How to get dazzling mileage out of paint and paper clips – dangling Mexican-bright hearts are made from nothing more exotic than paper, paint and glue, while the spotted stars benefit from an ingenious halo of paper clips.

Making the Earrings

Hearts for Valentine's Day, stars for Christmas, diamonds if you can't afford the real thing — these earrings can be any shape you like and, thanks to their lightness, any size too.

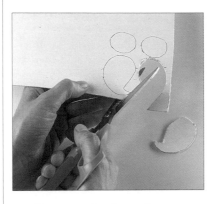  

1 Draw out the shape of your earrings on thick cardboard. Each of these earrings has two sections, a small circular shape for the top of the earring, and a comma shape that will hang from this. Cut out the shapes with scissors.

2 Using a matchstick, apply rapid epoxy resin to each earring shape and glue an earring finding on each so that the loop of the finding overlaps the edge in each case. These findings will be used to hook the top and bottom shapes together. Leave them to dry for one to two hours.

3 Tear two layers of newsprint into strips 5cm (2in) long and 2.5cm (1in) wide. Mix up a small amount of wallpaper paste according to the manufacturer's instructions. Dip one strip at a time into the paste, then paste it over the cardboard shapes and smooth it down. Cover both sides of each shape, then leave them on a cake rack to dry overnight. Repeat the whole process.

4 Having checked they are dry, paint the earring shapes on both sides with a coat of white emulsion paint and leave to dry. The paint will provide a better surface than newsprint for decorating the earrings.

5 To attach the earring sections together, prise open the finding on the bottom section with pliers and hook this through the finding loop on the top section. Bend back the hook to close it and secure it with rapid epoxy resin.

Decorating the Earrings

*Paint, sweet wrappers and gemstones make these
show-stoppers. You could experiment with gold leaf for
class, or Christmas glitter for kitsch.*

Coloured foil

**Flat-backed
gemstones**

MATERIALS
Gouache paints
Rapid epoxy resin
Flat-backed
gemstones
*(available from
craft shops)*
Coloured foil
Clear gloss
polyurethane
varnish

EQUIPMENT
Artist's brush
Matchstick
Scissors
Newspaper

1 *Using gouache paints, paint
different-coloured stripes on both
sides of the earrings to cover the white
emulsion completely. This will provide
the background colour to the earrings.
Leave to dry.*

2 *Applying rapid epoxy resin with
a matchstick, glue several flat-
backed gemstones onto the front of
each earring. Use a variety of different
colours and sizes of gemstones for
a dazzling effect. Leave to dry.*

3 *Cut strips of coloured foil about
6mm (¼in) wide. Using a
matchstick, apply rapid epoxy resin
around one gemstone at a time.
Position a strip of foil on the glued
area around the gemstone, pushing it
into place carefully with your fingers
as you go. Cut off any spare foil.
Repeat the process for each gemstone.*

4 *For extra sparkle, paint the edges
of each earring with gold gouache
paint. Leave to dry for approximately
half an hour.*

5 *Using rapid epoxy resin, glue an
earring fastening to the back of
each earring. Leave to dry until the
fastenings are firmly fixed.*

6 *Holding the earrings by their back
fastenings, dip them into a tin
of clear gloss polyurethane varnish to
coat them completely. Lay them on
newspaper and leave to dry. The
varnish gives the earrings extra shine
and a protective coat.*

Precious Paper

MATERIALS

Toilet paper
Water
Casein paint or gesso

EQUIPMENT

Kebab sticks or
knitting needles
Bowl
Jam jar
Cake tin (optional)
Artist's brush

See p.76 for materials
to decorate the beads.

SUBTLE GLINTS OF COLOUR and gold, as smoothly faceted as the opalescent interior of an oyster's shell – these lustrous baubles are child's play to make, and look sumptuous in generous swags as the sole and sophisticated adornment of a simple black dress. The technique could not be easier, and the resulting beads can be ornate or plain, smooth or textured, shiny or matt, slender tubes or dumpy spheres.

You could paint them with loose dashes of colour, as here, or with fine detail using acrylic or gouache and a small sable brush. Try painting dots, stripes or zigzags in bright rainbows, or in one or two colours to match an outfit. You could stipple your beads like a quail's egg, or emboss them with a matchstick and give them the aged look of verdigris with green and turquoise. Thread your beads on fine, shiny silk twine, a coloured leather thong knotted between each bead, or hemp string to link beads of black, cinnabar and gold.

Sumptuous Baubles
If you are of the school of thought that believes big is best, and lots is even better when it comes to finery, then a king's ransom of papier mâché baubles is for you.

Spangle Power
Raid the rainbow, add silver and gold, and you have an unbeatable recipe for visual riches. Who needs diamonds when all the colour in the world is at the tip of your paintbrush?

Making the Beads

So simple a child could do it, and so effective that an adult might just have a go – beads of all sizes and shapes are the work of a moment.

1 *Wrap a length of toilet paper around a kebab stick or knitting needle several times, and then dip it into a bowl of water and squeeze out as much as possible, shaping the bead as you go. Push the bead down the stick and repeat the process with another length of paper. When you have four beads on the stick, place the stick in a jam jar and leave the beads to dry. Alternatively, speed up the drying time considerably by slipping the beads off the stick and putting them in a cake tin in an oven at a very low setting. Check them every ten minutes or so.*

2 *Mix up casein paint to the consistency of double cream. Paint this onto the beads to cover them completely and leave to dry. The casein paint will provide a smooth surface to paint on. You could also paint the beads with gesso for a similar finish.*

Decorating the Beads

A chance to run wild with colour and gold leaf – take inspiration from textiles or embroidery.

Silver Dutch metal leaf

Gold Dutch metal leaf

MATERIALS
Opaque, pearlescent
and transparent acrylic inks
Transparent watercolour ink
Gold and silver poster paint
High-gloss clear polyurethane varnish
Silver and gold Dutch metal leaf
Cord or leather thonging

EQUIPMENT
Artist's brush
Varnish brush

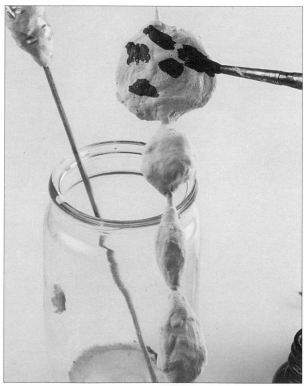

1 *Using coloured acrylic inks – opaque, pearlescent and transparent – daub dots of colour onto the beads.*

2 *Gradually cover the entire surface of the beads with dots and strokes of colour, building up the effect using opaque then pearlescent and then transparent ink, overlaying different colours. Allow the beads to dry.*

3 *Next paint the beads with sepia transparent watercolour ink to tone down the bright colours of the acrylic ink and create an antiquing effect. Leave the beads to dry for a few minutes.*

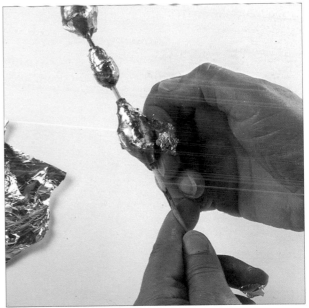

4 *Smudge gold and silver poster paint on the beads with a semi-dry brush, allowing the base colours to show through. Leave the beads to dry, then apply two to five coats of polyurethane gloss varnish, allowing each coat to dry before applying the next.*

5 *Press small torn pieces of silver and gold Dutch metal leaf onto the beads, pressing and smoothing out with the ball of the thumb. Finally apply another coat of varnish for a high-gloss finish and allow to dry. To make the beads up into a necklace, twist them off the stick, carefully smoothing away any rough edges where the hole passes through the bead, and thread them onto a length of cord or leather thonging.*

Copper-stemmed Vase

MATERIALS

Medium-weight
cardboard
Masking tape
Flour
Water
Newsprint

EQUIPMENT

Metal ruler
Scissors
Protractor
Pencil
String

See p.80 for materials
to decorate the vase.

A VASE THAT FLOATS on its own copper curlicue, an elegant tapered cone vibrant with the partnership of indigo outside and a gleaming metallic throat within, would make the perfect receptacle for a swathe of peacocks' feathers or fronds of airy dried flowers. But the more ambitious or adventurous – with ready access to a soldering iron – can make a tremulous, glittering bouquet of brass stars and hearts, leaves and teardrops, fixed to copper wire, which will shiver and twinkle with every breath of wind.

This vase, whose uneven shadowed and shining surface shows off the inimitable richness of metal leaf, uses a simply constructed foundation of cardboard, while loose pigment gives it the velvety depth of colour. The result is a beautiful object, delicate and elegant, like an upturned datura flower. A pair of them would make a graceful adjunct to a mantelpiece, while different sizes in harmonizing shades of one colour would make a handsome group.

Velvet Colour

Elegance in triplicate, the use of loose powder pigment gives an astonishing matt richness of colour to these vases, in contrast to the swirl of a copper stem and the gleaming metal leaf.

Precious Metal Bowl

Nothing beats metal leaf for a glamorous transformation. Applying it is not difficult to do, rather it is fiddly, but you will soon be hooked and find yourself casting about for objects to gild. Gold, silver and copper look decadently opulent together.

Making the Vase

The smooth and elegant line of this vase is easy to achieve. As you become more proficient you can experiment with different basic shapes.

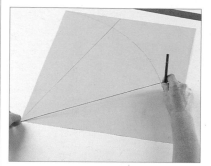 

1 *Cut a piece of cardboard 42cm (16½ in) square. To make the curved shape, measure 25° at the top left corner of the cardboard using a protractor, and mark with a pencil. Tie a piece of string onto the end of the pencil. With one hand, hold the pencil upright on the mark in the top left corner. With the other hand, pull the string taut and hold the end over the bottom left corner. Draw a curved edge from the top left corner to the bottom right corner of the cardboard.*

2 *Cut along the curved edge. Roll the cardboard between your hands to make a cone shape. The cardboard will have a double thickness. Stick strips of masking tape along the edge to keep the cone shape. Finally, secure further by sticking a piece of tape down the entire length of the join.*

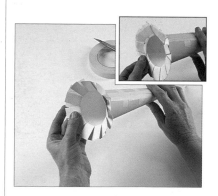 

3 *Using scissors, make cuts about 3cm (1¼ in) long into the top of the cone, taking each layer of cardboard individually. Leave gaps of 1.5cm (⅝ in) between cuts. Fold the cut ends down to form the rim of the vase. Place small strips of masking tape around the top and underside of the rim to strengthen it and make it even (see inset).*

4 *Make up the paste by whisking 1 tablespoon flour and 315ml (10fl oz) water over a gentle heat until the mixture begins to boil. Allow to cool. Paste small strips of newsprint inside the vase to a depth of 7.5cm (3in). Then cover the outside with overlapping paper strips, and paste two layers over the rim. Leave the edges around the rim rough. Allow to dry overnight.*

Decorating the Vase

MATERIALS
Gesso
Pink acrylic paint
Cobalt blue powdered pigment
Fixative
Purple soft artist's pastel
Red oxide primer
Gold size
Copper Dutch metal leaf
Metallic bronze powder
1.5m (62in) copper microbore tubing, 5mm (¾ in) thick
Brass fencing
Thin copper wire

EQUIPMENT
Paintbrush
Cotton wool
Scissors
Fork
Soldering iron

1 *Apply two coats of gesso both inside and outside the vase to stiffen the cardboard and give a textured surface. When dry, apply a coat of pink acrylic paint to the outside of the vase and leave to dry again.*

2 *Using a pad of cotton wool, dab blue powdered pigment over the entire surface of the vase. Rub it for an interesting effect. Spray the vase with fixative to fix the pigment in place, taking care not to inhale any. This will dry almost immediately.*

3 *Rub a purple soft artist's pastel over the rim of the vase and smear it with your fingers to create patches of intense colour. Spray with fixative to fix the pastel.*

4 *Paint the inside of the vase with red oxide primer and allow to dry thoroughly. Apply a thin, even coat of gold size to the inside and the rim and leave for approximately 30 minutes until it squeaks when rubbed with a finger. Lay pieces of copper Dutch metal leaf onto the size, blowing on it to make it lie flat if necessary, then smooth it down with your fingers. Afterwards, rub off any excess with your fingers.*

5 *Dip a pad of cotton wool into metallic bronze powder, then tap the pad over the vase so that the dust drops inside the vase to coat the size. Be careful to protect your surfaces as metallic powder gets everywhere. Continue the process until the size is covered with bronze dust. Then spray fixative inside the vase to fix the metallic powder in place.*

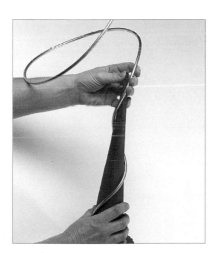

6 *Take the copper microbore tubing and, holding the top of it tightly in one hand, coil it around the vase twice. Then coil the other end of the tubing to make a flat base for the vase so that it stands upright.*

7 *To make the copper stems cut out decorative shapes, such as circles, hearts, leaves, teardrops and stars, from a piece of brass fencing. Press down hard with the end of a fork into the surface of each brass shape to make patterned indentations.*

8 *Take a strip of thin copper wire 70cm (28in) long. Lay it on a brass shape and solder the two together using a hot soldering iron (follow the manufacturer's instructions). Repeat until you have several copper stems with a brass shape at the end of each. These stems can be inserted in the vase.*

Bole Bowl

MATERIALS

Clingfilm
Newsprint
Rabbit skin glue
Water
Rabbit skin gesso

EQUIPMENT

Bowl for mould
Bain marie
Paintbrush
Silicon carbide paper

See p.84 for materials
to decorate the bowl.

THIS MAGNIFICENT BOWL is a virtuoso exercise in skill and patience, using traditional methods and materials to achieve a finish of professional marble-smoothness. The artist who made this huge container, which measures 38cm (15¼in) in diameter, demonstrates a fluent expertise that is the result of much experience. The finished object is not too difficult to make, although it requires a bit of uninterrupted dedication.

Its cool tactile perfection is owed to multiple coats of rabbit skin gesso applied to a simple layered base. The final result is heavier and more substantial than plain papier mâché, and the gesso completely obliterates the bowl's humble newspaper origins. Subtle shades of Wedgwood blue and slate-brown pigment were applied using a fine clay, known as bole, adding another layer to the refinement of the surface texture. Finally, this sophisticated piece was given a touch of water gilding, whose initial harsh glare was muted with a magical trick of alchemy relying on nothing more mysterious than a hard-boiled egg. This is a piece to work up to, and one of which you can feel jubilantly proud when complete.

Black Beauty

This is a bowl that invites a caress – all that patient work with layers of gesso gives a seductive solidity and elegant smoothness to the finish. The combination of polished bole and antiqued silver is about as grand as paper can aspire to.

Gesso Finesse
Humble beginnings transformed in a small miracle of skill – vary colour and motif as you will, paper and gesso combined with finesse result in pure sophistication.

Making the Bowl

Probably the most demanding project in the book, this bowl is not quick to make, and requires a certain perfectionism in the finish, but the result is in a league of its own.

1 *Cover a mould with clingfilm. Then paste about 10 layers of long paper strips over the clingfilm, from top to bottom, using rabbit skin glue. To prepare the glue, mix 1 part rabbit skin glue with 10 parts water. Gently heat in a bain marie until the glue is hot. Leave the bowl to dry, then remove from the mould.*

2 *Paint rabbit skin gesso onto the outside of the paper bowl and then the inside and leave to dry. Repeat until you have applied between 10 and 20 layers – the more layers of gesso you paint on, the better the finish will be. Allow each coat to dry before applying the next one.*

3 *Using silicon carbide paper, sand the surface of the bowl to remove any bumps and unevenness, until it feels as smooth as porcelain.*

Decorating the Bowl

The dark lustre of bole makes a magnificent foil for the interesting alchemy of ancient silver conjured with an egg.

MATERIALS
Blue bole
Rabbit skin glue
Blue-brown bole mix
Brown bole
Tracing paper
Low-tack tape
Water mixed with
methylated spirits
Silver leaf
Hard-boiled egg
Superfine white polish

EQUIPMENT
Nylon tights
Soft paintbrush
Fine-grade wire wool
Scissors
Pencil
Gilding mop
Gilder's tip
Cotton wool
Agate burnisher

1 *Prepare the bole (a fine clay) by mixing 1 heaped teaspoon with a little rabbit skin glue (which should be no warmer than blood temperature) until the mixture is the thickness of single cream. Strain through nylon tights. Using a soft brush, apply three coats of blue bole onto the bowl, brushing quickly. Then apply one or two coats of blue-brown bole and finally a coat of brown bole.*

2 *When the bowl has dried, take a pad of fine-grade wire wool and rub it over the surface of the bowl to give it a soft sheen.*

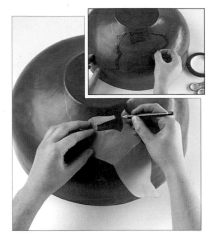

3 *Cut out decorative shapes from tracing paper – here, different animals – and draw around the shape on the outside of the bowl using a pencil. These shapes will then be gilded on the bowl. Stick small pieces of low-tack tape around the edge of the drawn shape on the bowl to mask off the edge of the area to be gilded (see inset).*

4 *Using a gilding mop (squirrel-hair brush), brush water mixed with a drop of methylated spirits over the surface of the shape to be gilded, keeping within the mask. The water will bring the rabbit skin glue in the gesso to the surface of the bowl, enabling the silver leaf to adhere.*

5 *Working quickly and using a gilder's tip, lay a piece of silver leaf carefully on the wet surface of the bowl. Tap it into position with a soft brush. Repeat to cover all the area to be gilded, then leave to dry.*

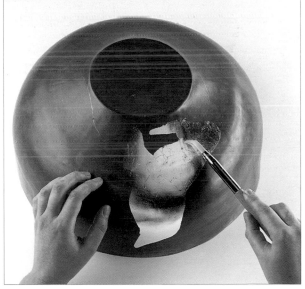

6 *Rub the surface of the silver leaf with a ball of cotton wool to smooth it down and rub off any overlapping pieces. Carefully remove the low-tack tape from around the edges and the gilded shape will be revealed.*

7 *Burnish the gilded areas with an agate burnisher. This presses the silver leaf down securely, smooths out any creases and brings out the shine. For further decorative effect, place the bowl upside-down over a chopped, newly hard-boiled egg. The sulphur from the egg will tarnish and mottle the silver leaf. Seal the bowl with superfine white polish, applied with a soft brush. Rub the surface with fine-grade wire wool, then apply a final layer of polish.*

Festive Star Bowl

MATERIALS
Balloon
Cardboard
String
Newsprint
PVA glue
Water
Gold mirror paper
Red acetate
Parchment
Water-based gloss
varnish

EQUIPMENT
Plate
Scissors
Scalpel
Flowerpot
Housepainter's brush
Pencil
Varnish brush

THE TECHNIQUE OF INSERTING coloured acetate in rich stained glass colours into papier mâché is an original one, and would lend itself (with all due precautions) to making lanterns from which a nightlight could twinkle. Put one on a windowsill to welcome winter visitors, or in summer you could hang one from a tree to bring star-spangled enchantment to your garden. Or you could simply use it as a decoration, piled high with Christmas baubles.

The red stars could be replaced by simple geometric cut-outs in rainbow colours for a child's room, or narrow strips of brilliant blue in a black and silver ground for a more sophisticated look. The combination of opaque and transparent colour begs to be shown off in changing lights: placed on a sunny windowsill, the bowls cast stars upon the paintwork; by candlelight, they have a mysterious glow.

Christmas Stars
The white and gold of this bowl are decidedly celebratory colours, while the sprinkling of transparent scarlet stars adds to the feeling of Christmas. Make a bunch of them to grace a winter windowsill.

1 *Make a layered bowl using a balloon as a mould (see p.30) Rip the top edge all around to create an undulating rim. Make a star template from cardboard and draw around this all over the outside of the paper bowl. Then, using a scalpel, cut out the star shapes from the outside.*

2 *Bind the cut edges with small strips of gold mirror paper or foil, wrapping the paper from the outside to the inside of the bowl. Add a small strip across each point of the star on the outside of the bowl, so that each star is completely surrounded with gold.*

3 *Using PVA glue, paste pieces of red acetate over the inside of each cut-out star. Hold the acetate in position with a weight while it dries. Then paste torn strips of parchment on the outside of the bowl, leaving a narrow gold edging around each star, and small strips of gold mirror paper on the inside. Paint the bowl with a coat of dilute PVA to seal the surface, then varnish it inside and out with water-based gloss varnish.*

Ideas to Inspire

With the basics of making and moulding under your belt, let your creative side take over and go wild with paint, powders, threads and jewels, or anything else you fancy. Keep your eyes open and you will find a use for feathers and glitter, shiny cord and patterned shells, copper wire and pieces of frosted glass.

▶ **Stitched Up**
Constructed from paper pulp, this bowl was decorated with stitched fabric and paper, and string arches covered with gold tissue paper, then rubbed with boot polish for an aged effect.

▶ **Calligraphy Bowl**
Created by a lettering artist who uses papier mâché as a vehicle for her lettering, this bowl has a smooth finish, made by layering over a glass mould and sanding with an electric sander.

◀ **Medieval Casket**
Medieval church ornamentation was the inspiration for this casket, which was made from cardboard decorated with string, cardboard shapes and beads. It was painted with emulsion and poster paints, then varnished and sponged with gold acrylic.

▲ Zebra Clock

Constructed simply from a cardboard frame and layers of paper, this clock would add a touch of humour to any mantelpiece. It was painted with acrylics and emulsion, and Japanese papers were glued on for contrast. The zebra was modelled from pulp and glued on.

◀ Pedestal Bowl

The pedestal of this bowl was formed by rolling up strips of PVA-covered newsprint into a tube shape and, when dry, pasting this to the bowl. The bowl was painted with acrylics, sponged with gold gouache paint and decorated with collage before being varnished.

▲ Statuesque Cupboard

Measuring 1.8m (6ft) tall, this impressive cupboard was constructed from pulp applied over a plywood framework. Wavy lines, dots, triangles and swirls of pulp were added for relief decoration. The cupboard was sponged with acrylic paint and decorated with coloured foil, while the relief decoration was gilded.

◄ Painted Tissue Clock

This clock was created by first decorating tissue paper with dry pigment colours, metallic powders, acrylics and oil paints.

When dry, layers of painted tissue were applied onto a piece of hardboard cut into the desired shape. Inserting the clock mechanism is a straightforward process.

▼ Spiky Frame

The surface of this unusually shaped frame, made from a cardboard base covered with newsprint, was decorated with paint, coloured tissue, cartridge and sugar paper. Pieces of broken mirror were glued onto the frame and highlights were picked out in gold leaf.

◀ Chunky Bangle
Constructed by layering paper over a twisted length of newsprint joined in a circle, this bangle was decorated with gold paint, foil and gemstones.

◀ Exotic Earrings
Made from paper pulp, these earrings were sealed with acrylic gesso then decorated with metallic, gouache and watercolour paints and metallic powder, before being given a coat of varnish.

▶ Dazzling Display
These decorative pieces were constructed by layering paper over a cardboard framework. The elephant on the box lid was made using a modelling clay mould. Both the cupboard and box were painted with gouache paints and decorated with small circular shisha mirrors before being varnished.

Templates

*Shown here are the templates for two of the projects featured
earlier in the book. Enlarge the templates to the required size
on a photocopier, keeping all the templates from one project in
proportion to each other.*

Tricorn Vase
(p.24)

Kitsch Casket
(p.52)

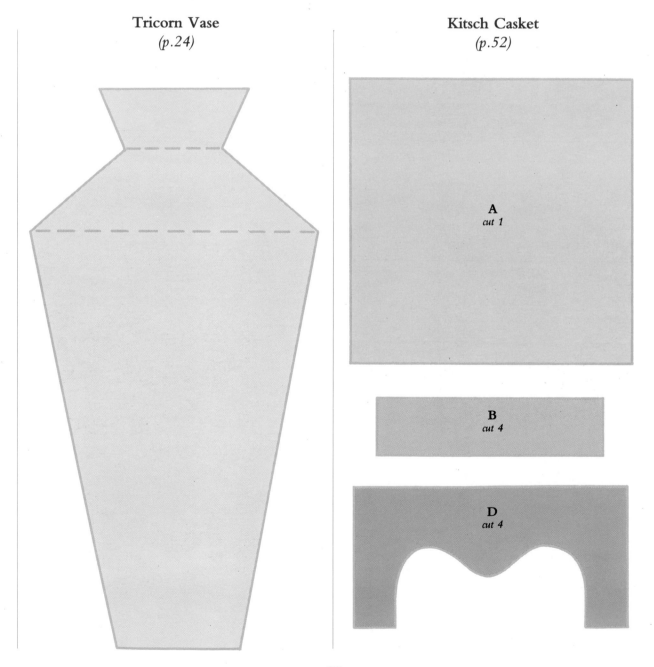

A
cut 1

B
cut 4

D
cut 4

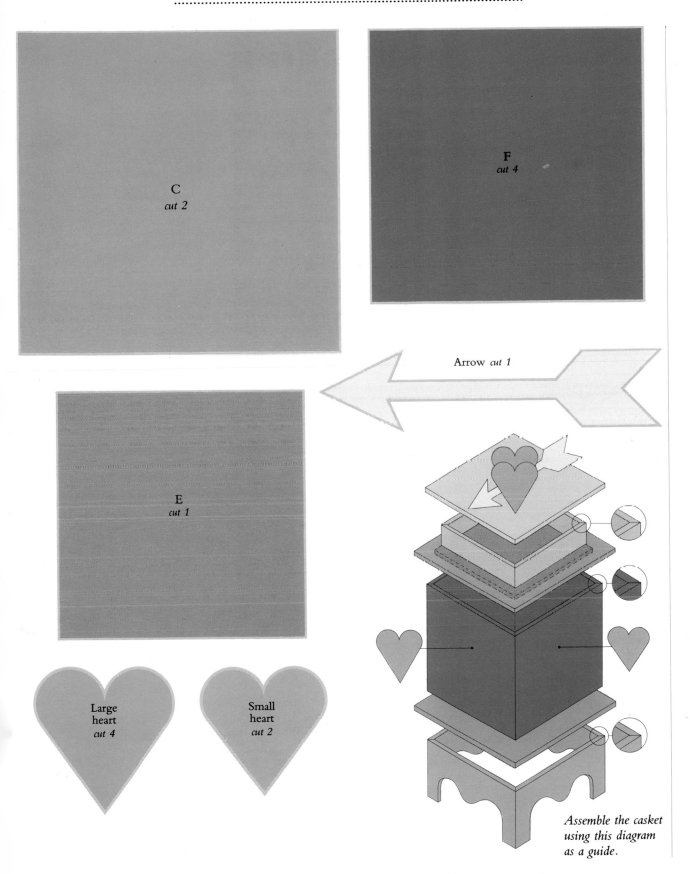

C
cut 2

F
cut 4

Arrow *cut 1*

E
cut 1

Large
heart
cut 4

Small
heart
cut 2

*Assemble the casket
using this diagram
as a guide.*

Contributors

Madeleine Adams
Urn (pp.32-33); bowls (p.35 top); lidded box (pp.48-51)
Tel: 01608 684661
Cobweb Cottage
Stourton Hill
Nr Shipston on Stour
Warwickshire CV36 5HH

Julie Arkell
Earrings (pp.70-73); bangle (p.91)
Tel: 0171-916 6447
Unit W8
Cockpit Yard Workshops
Northington Street
London WC1N 2NP

Rhoda Baker
Frame (p.61 top)
Tel: 01273 676761
Colourbox
3 Upper Wellington Road
Brighton
East Sussex BN2 3AN

Hilary Bravo
Bowl (pp.28-31); beads (pp.74-77)
Tel: 01981 240883
Cobblers Grove
Pontrilas
Herefordshire HR2 0BL

Patrick Burton
Clock (p.90)
Tel: 0171-703 3393
3 Urlwin Street
London SE5 0NF

Ann Carter
Fish box (p.62 centre); tray (pp.66-69)
Tel: 01993 702335
15 Church Green
Witney
Oxfordshire OX8 6AZ

Tim Chesters/Diana Longenberg (Chameleons)
Clock (p.61)
Tel: 01273 772793
Top Flat
61 Church Street
Brighton
East Sussex BN1 3LF

Gerry Copp
Clock (pp.40-43)
Tel: 01522 730218
School Cottage
Ainthorpe
Lincoln LN1 2SG

Hazel Dolby
Bowl (p.88 centre)
Tel: 01420 588311
Deanyers Cottage
Hall Lane
Farringdon, Alton
Hampshire GU34 3EA

Hannah Downes
Frame (p.63)
Tel: 0171-585 2131
37a Vardens Road
London SW11 1RQ

Margaret Frere-Smith
Cockerel (p.63)
Tel: 01502 578421
Whitehouse Farmhouse
Uggeshall, Nr Beccles
Suffolk NR34 8BJ

Ann Frith
Cupboard (p.89)
Tel: 01273 625365
5 Chesham Street
Kemptown, Brighton
East Sussex BN2 1NA

Martin Hall
Vase (pp.24-27)
Tel: 01273 326766
41b Norfolk Square
Brighton
East Sussex BN1 2PE

Carol Hill
Bowl (pp.12-15); bowl (pp.16-19); bowls (p.36 bottom)
Tel: 01306 882017
Arcadia
Cotmandene, Dorking
Surrey RH4 2BN

Kim & Di Hincks
Dish (pp.20-23); casket (pp.52-55); wall cupboard (p.91); box (p.91)
Tel: 0116 700229
36 Portland Road
Stoneygate
Leicester LE2 3AB

Kim Homer
Bowls (p.37)
Tel: 01293 511170
11 Latimer Close
Langley Green
Crawley
West Sussex RH11 7SJ

Julie Howells
Bowls (p.36); earrings (p.91)
Tel: 01344 773866
35 Greenwood Road
Crowthorne
Berkshire RG11 6JS

Sarah Kelly
Plate (p.35 bottom); goldfish (p.62 bottom right); bowl (pp.86-87)
Tel: 01273 381704
43 North Gardens
Brighton
East Sussex BN1 3LB

Alice Leach
Bowl (pp.82-85)
Tel: 0181-746 0387
57 Pennard Road
London W12 8DW

Rosemary Mackinder
Bowl (p.88 top)
Tel: 01777 701919
2 Savile Street
Retford
Nottinghamshire DN22 6ET

Joanne McCrum
Bowls (p.34 and p.35 bottom left); vases (p.60)
Tel: 01396 821168
6 Plantation Street
Killyleagh, Downpatrick
Co Down BT30 9QN
Northern Ireland

Julie Mosley
Chest (p.61)
Tel: 0161-962 0650
38 Coppice Avenue
Sale, Cheshire M33 4WB

Jennie Neame
Curtained mirror (pp.44-47)
Tel: 0171-278 3045
15 Stanley Buildings
Pancras Road
London NW1 2TD

Glynis Porter
Clock (p.89)
Tel: 0181-747 0469
12 Gainsborough Road
London W4 1NJ

Carolyn Sansbury
Bowl (p.2); vase (pp.78-81)
Tel: 01273 735804
12B Powis Square
Brighton
East Sussex BN1 3HG

Eleanor Staley
Casket (p.88)
Tel: 01684 574392
32 St Ann's Road
Great Malvern
Worcestershire WR14 4RG

Yanina Temple
Bowl (p.89); frame (p.90)
Tel: 01509 218160
15 York Road
Loughborough
Leicestershire LE11 3DA

Jan Tricker
Frame (p.61 bottom)
Dolphin House
18 Hale Street
Staines
Middlesex TW18 4UW

John Tutton/Sarah Young (Odyssey)
Mask (p.56); toy bug (p.62); fish plaques (p.62 bottom right and p.63)
Tel: 01273 720486
31 Norfolk Square
Brighton
East Sussex BN1 2PE

Melanie Williams
Dolls (p.60)
Tel: 01874 711826
Bronllys Castle
Bronllys
Powys LD3 0HL

Index

Acknowledgements

This book owes its inspiration to a thrilling crescendo of work which has recently brought a new vitality to craft exhibitions. The makers who participated in this book were extraordinarily generous – with their time and ideas – which is typical of their tribe, and makes them a rare and precious breed. People who make things are just much nicer than the rest of us! I am very grateful to everyone who contributed work; each piece is special in some way, and the torrent of jokey, whimsical and appealing creativity is wonderfully cheering in a world ruled by the strictures of profit and loss. Many thanks to Circus Arts in Brighton who were inspiring and so generous with loaning pieces for the book, and also to Stuart Stevenson who lent a wide range of paints and papers The Herculean labour of organizing and editing this book was the lot of Heather Dewhurst, who performed it with exemplary efficiency and calm. Steven Wooster transformed the raw material to make the elegant best of it, and Clive Streeter is a nonpareil among photographers. Congratulations to Marnie Searchwell for her inspired art direction and to Patrick Knowles for his contribution to the book. Finally, Colin Ziegler is always a pleasure to work with.